THE STRATEGIC DIALOGUE

THE STRATEGIC DIALOGUE

Rendering the Diagnostic Interview a Real Therapeutic Intervention

Giorgio Nardone

and

Alessandro Salvini

Routledge
Taylor & Francis Group

LONDON AND NEW YORK

First published 2007 by Karnac Books Ltd

Published 2018 by Routledge
2 Park Square, Milton Park, Abingdon, Oxon OX14 4RN
711 Third Avenue, New York, NY 10017, USA

Routledge is an imprint of the Taylor & Francis Group, an informa business

British Library Cataloguing in Publication Data

A C.I.P. for this book is available from the British Library

ISBN 978 1 85575 556 7 (pbk)

Edited, designed and produced by The Studio Publishing Services Ltd, www.publishingservicesuk.co.uk
E-mail: studio@publishingservicesuk.co.uk

CONTENTS

ABOUT THE AUTHORS   vii

PREFACE by Paul Watzlawick   ix

INTRODUCTION by Giorgio Nardone   xi

CHAPTER ONE
Discovering the forgotten   1

CHAPTER TWO
The structure of the strategic dialogue   33

CHAPTER THREE
The strategic dialogue in action: examples of
technological magic   49

CHAPTER FOUR
A dialogue on the dialogue   103

REFERENCES   113

INDEX   119

Giorgio Nardone is Director of Centro di Terapia Strategica (Strategic Therapy Centre) and of the Post Graduate School of Brief Strategic Therapy Centre in Arezzo. He is also Professor of Brief Psychotherapy at the Post Graduate School of Clinical Psychology, University of Siena, Italy. He has published numerous articles and several books, translated into many languages. He is renowned as one of the most creative therapists and authors in the field of brief strategic therapy and strategic problem-solving: his systematic and effective models for treating phobic–obsessive disorders and eating disorders are followed by many psychotherapists all around the world. Details of his publications can be found at: http://www. giorgionardone.it/bibliography.asp

Alessandro Salvini is a clinical psychologist. He teaches psycho-pathology and clinical psychology at the University of Padova (General Psychology Department). He has focused his research on the exploration of dissociative personality processes, clinical psychology, new models of psychotherapy in a transcultural pers-pective, gender disturbances, diversity and deviances, states of con-sciousness, and inner voices experiences. He is currently involved in the Brief Strategic Therapy Training School (Brief Strategic Therapy Training MRI Model) and is an active member of the Centre for Strategic Therapy, Arezzo.

PREFACE

It is with great pleasure that I present this masterwork, which I consider to be a fundamental contribution to the evolution of brief therapy.

The strategic dialogue, as defined by the authors, is in fact the synthesis of the evolution of ancient rhetoric and modern pragmatism in communication, the noble Art of Stratagems and the application of Ericksonian hypotheses to the clinical field.

Further gratification derives from the fact that Giorgio Nardone, with whom I had the pleasure of working for more than fifteen years, until my retirement from my profession, and with whom I founded the Centre of Strategic Therapy in Arezzo, has been able once more to develop new ideas and to put together further original therapeutic techniques, which render this work both innovative and seminal.

Moreover, one should not ignore the fact that Nardone was responsible for turning the Institute in Arezzo into an international point of reference in the scientific advancement of brief therapy, thanks to the research work and clinical application carried out together with his always expanding group of collaborators around the globe.

This work embraces the participation of Professor Alessandro Salvini, who presents an elegant and refined, yet highly efficient and effective technique to help people break away from their pathological traps.

Through a seemingly simple and thus disarming dialogue, structured on the bases of certain elaborated and subtle techniques, the first session becomes a complete and effective therapy.

As stated in the text, the therapeutic power of the strategic dialogue resides in its "surprising essentiality" or, better, in guiding persons entrapped in their problems to come to discover the solution in a sort of natural and spontaneous evolution throughout the therapeutic conversation.

Thanks to an elaborated yet subtle communicative expedient, the patient feels as if he is the main protagonist and artefact of the therapeutic change.

While reading through the full transcriptions of the cases presented, readers will immerse themselves fully in Giorgio Nardone's style of work, and will be fascinated by the articulate dialogue, carried out through the use of precise strategic plans that are adaptable both to the structure of the problem and also to the peculiar reality of the patient. Moreover, the reader will be astonished to discover how, through the use of subtle communicative manoeuvres and creative stratagems, patients are led to rapid, as well as effective, therapeutic change.

Thus, I believe that this text is a "must read", not only for therapists, but also for all those interested in the study of communication and its therapeutic effects who, while going through its pages, will uncover a sort of "magical code".

As a final point, I would like to underline the fact that this work is not only a treatise related to a particular psychotherapeutic model, but is also the explication of a school of thought that takes up, in a disillusive and pragmatic way, the complexity relative to how we relate with ourselves, others, and the world and how, through such a complex network of interrelations, we construct or, more accurately, invent, our own realities.

Paul Watzlawick
Palo Alto, 2007

Introduction

Giorgio Nardone

This book represents both the starting and finishing line of all of the research, clinical practice, and managerial consulting performed by professors Giorgio Nardone and Paul Watzlawick over a fifteen-year period at the Centre of Strategic Therapy in Arezzo (Centro di Terapia Strategica di Arezzo). This work is the result of the combined efforts and contributions of not only the authors of this book, but also of other colleagues, collaborators, scholars, and patients from all over the world, many of whom were often unaware of the help they provided during our dialogues.

This work can be referred to as the finishing line of our work because the strategic dialogue, an advanced therapeutic method of conducting a therapy session and inducing radical changes rapidly in the patient, represents the culmination of all that has been achieved so far in the field. The strategic dialogue is a fine strategy by which *one can achieve maximum results with minimum effort*. It was developed through a natural evolutionary process from previous treatments for particular pathologies, and is composed of therapeutic stratagems and specific sequences of *ad hoc* manoeuvres constructed for different types of problems. It was through the dramatically efficient and effective successes of these therapeutic protocols that we devised the strategic dialogue, and turned the first therapy session into a true change-inducing intervention rather than a mere preliminary "diagnostic" or "assessment" phase. Thus the "assessment" questions became very strategic, the therapist's paraphrasing became highly reframing, and the language became highly evocative of sensations in order to produce immediate change in the patient even as the therapist was "merely assessing" the problem in the first session. Finally, the therapeutic prescriptions, homework typically given by a strategic therapist at the end of a session, became the spontaneous evolution of the dialogue, not just an abrupt assignment bearing no obvious relation to the presenting problem, as patients sometimes perceive. In this way, by *knowing a problem through its solution*, a constructivist method of research, the logical operative and strategic means of conducting the first, and often only, therapy session, emerged. It should be noted that while we use the terms therapy session and patient, the same method also applies to managerial consultancy encounters and coaching clients.

On the other hand, this book is also a starting point. The establishment of, and experimentation with, the strategic dialogue has opened up new and promising prospects for research and intervention concerning its power to promote change and its application to different contexts. From our point of view, all of this is due to a method that induces change, not as the product of the "expert's" directives to the "inexpert", but rather as the result of a joint discovery of two individuals through a dialogue that was purposely structured to fulfil this objective.

In this way, we completely nullify the natural resistance present in all individual or extended human systems, which tends to oppose any changes that might alter the discomforting and pathological equilibrium. In fact, by using the strategic dialogue, we can transform a limit into a resource. The therapist, just like a wise strategist, can use very subtle manoeuvres to guide his patient into feeling like the main protagonist of the scene; and in this way the latter becomes more easily persuaded of what he has come to feel and discover.

We believe that the "magic" of this technique resides in its *innate quality*, consistent with the Wisdoms of the Hellenic tradition: not too much, just enough.

CHAPTER ONE

Discovering the forgotten

"One should not violate nature but persuade it"

(Epicurus, in Messner Loebs, 2003)

In *The Philosophy of Santayana* (1950), Bertrand Russell presents Santayana's proposal to discover the forgotten, based on the idea that there is "nothing new under these skies if not the forgotten". These words are very valid for the most modern, yet most ancient form of persuasive communication: *the dialogue*.

This is why we chose to start our exposition with a brief historical review regarding the use of the dialogue as an instrument of persuasion, in both written and verbal communication.

The use of this rhetorical device as a strategic technique has its roots in the history of civilization. The etymological meaning of the word dialogue, *dia-logos*, is a discourse between two; the exchange or encounter of intelligence (Von Foerster, 1993), referring to an act of communication through which a new knowledge is acquired, and coming to discover together something more than that which one could ever discover alone. It is not by chance that the dialogue is the most used expository form in scientific, religious, and philosophical dissertations, of both the Western and Eastern cultures.

One has merely to recall the telling dialogue between God and Satan, mentioned by the first biblical Christian prophets, where the devil induces God to torture Job, his most loyal believer, to test his true devotion.

In reviewing the history of mankind, we discover the power of the dialogue in its various forms, perhaps representing the most used rhetorical device in the chronicles of human reason. In fact, we will try to demonstrate that this persuasive expedient has been used by the most famous of thinkers. These great minds, despite fierce opposition, managed to spread their ideas and convince others of their validity, thanks to the efficiency and effectiveness of the dialogue itself. According to our point of view, this implies that the dialogue represents an extraordinarily persuasive instrument, and we shall present evidence of the incredible power of this rhetorical stratagem.

The first to make use of the dialogue as a persuasive technique was Protagoras, the principal proponent of Hellenic sophistry in ancient Greece. As Master of Wisdom, Protagoras made use of the so-called Eristic dialogue (*eristikè tèchne*—i.e., the art of argumentation), aimed to persuade the interlocutor of his thesis (Abbagnano, 1993; Volpi, 1991). The form of this dialogue was an art founded more on putting forward questions rather than that of proposing answers. These questions were structured in a particular successive order to elicit certain responses from the interlocutor that would follow the desired direction of the persuader. The secret of this dialogue was for the sophist to change the convictions of the interlocutor by avoiding both coming into conflict with his convictions and using counter-arguments. Instead, the interlocutor is guided to discover alternatives through the use of the wisely chosen questions. This is carried out until the person comes to change his mind of his own accord, having been led by the sophist to contradict his own previously asserted assumptions. Through this process, the interlocutor becomes convinced that he himself was responsible for the new thesis that the two have come to agree upon, and not that this was imposed upon him by the persuader.

In this way, in Ancient Greece, the dialogue became a communication strategy that was elevated to a rhetorical technique, and thus it was included among those disciplines through which human beings, members of the new democratic state, ennobled themselves.

Sometimes this clever way of conducting the dialogue required a suggestive, somewhat "theatrical" capability. Protagoras, true genius that he was, had even created also a sort of scenography for when he needed to introduce himself to those who asked for his "expensive" services. When he was called to some nobleman's house, he always brought along a group of followers that formed a two-tailed queue behind him. As soon as Protagoras came to a stop, the followers would position themselves next to him to form a sort of theatrical tableau, and then go back to forming a queue as soon as he proceeded in his walk. From such an organization, one can understand that everything was studied in detail, even the non-verbal language and the scenographic effects.

It was a practical rather than just a theoretical knowledge, and Protagoras never disregarded its study or its dissemination. "Mastery", he maintained, "is the synthesis of natural predisposition and constant exercising." He was the first person to have taken up the study of the importance of words, metaphors, anti-logics, aphorisms, and the methods of argumentation using non-ordinary logic. He was a pupil of Democritus, the scholar who studied particles in nature. Democritus was the first to speak about the atom and its application to the study of linguistic particles and their use in the dialogue. Unfortunately, almost nothing is left of his writings, because his works, which numbered up to a hundred, were burned in the main square of Athens when he was accused of impiety (Diels & Kranz, 1934–1937). The accusations made led to the statement that man is the measure of all things; and that nobody could confirm whether or not the gods existed (Diogene Laerzio, IX). It was considered an unprejudiced philosophy because it was radically relativistic in nature and was in opposition to any form of orthodoxy or revealed truth. Protagoras had taught and practised a revealing relativism and not a moral relativism. He maintained that the wise man, when armed with the discourse and the dialectic, would manage to lead a person towards what was right and useful for his being and his becoming. His fine technique was alleged to be an illicit desire to lead a forged investigation of physical and moral problems. It was viewed as a source of religious scepticism and as an instrument of dishonest manipulation by means of sophistic artifice. However, what had happened to Protagoras had also happened to even his most famous rival, Socrates. The irony of fate would lead the two thinkers, though rivals in great contrast to one another, to the same condemnation: sentenced to death for impiety.

As affirmed by Gorge, another great sophist, the Protagoran dialogue was a useful instrument to convince the interlocutor of whichever thesis the Sophist desired.

It was Socrates who first proposed the *dialectic*. The dialectic is a dialogue orientated towards the search for the "truth", and this is quite independent of the individual's point of view. His technique consisted of embracing the argument of the interlocutor in a hypothetical form, and then using questions and answers to come to prove how these led to nothing, or to some absurd conclusion. The intent was to throw the interlocutor into confusion, while highlighting the invalidity of his argument and thus inducing him to search for the "truth". And yet, according to the ancient testimonies, when a young Socrates was invited by a friend to assist with one of Protagoras's performances, he ran out of arguments during the dispute and came close to physically attacking Protagoras. It is easy to understand why Socrates later began using the rhetorical techniques of Protagoras, even though he never really cited him, always professing great opposition to his ideas.

While Protagoras and the Sophists were erased from history, accused of having been mystifiers of the word, the Socratic method persisted and influenced Western thought. Nearly all philosophical thinking follows Socrates, since he was the initiator of the investigative method based on thinking. His famous affirmation "know thyself" endures as the foundation of the idea that to change something one needs to get to know it.

Thus began the historical–philosophical period of Rationalism. With it came the hypothesis that it is possible, through logical–rational procedures, to understand phenomena, to explain them, and, consequently, to intervene in them. This gave rise, together with Nietzsche, to what we could call "the rationalist illusion".

However, it might seem grotesque to reveal that it was actually Socrates who gave rise to the rationalist tradition. He is said to have been visited by a "demon" that inspired him with new arguments; in other words he heard "voices" which guided him: thus, his reasonableness was stirred from unreasonableness (Cioran, 1993).

As a consequence, he was either a "madman" believed to be a genius, or an impostor capable of using subtle stratagems to convince the Athenian people to give him credit that his thesis came from idolized divinities in the hereafter.

So, Socrates took up the rhetorical techniques of Protagoras, and transformed them into something totally different: a research instrument of truth within his own experience. The Socratic dialogue in this way became a "Maieutic" art (from the Greek word for midwife), for, just as the midwife helps mothers give birth to their children, the dialectic helps the individual get to know himself and the reality that surrounds him.

In line with the notion of the art of the Maieutic rather than the rhetorical, Socrates gave up writing in order to emphasize the unrepeatable nature of dialectic research. Socrates' literary silence was echoed by the writings of his disciple, Plato, who none the less wrote in the form of a dialogue. The Platonic dialogues held a persuasive force that influenced the philosophies that followed him.

Even though Plato officially claimed to be a loyal disciple and follower of Socrates' teachings, in his dialogues he did not hesitate to go beyond the doctrinal legacy of his Master. He wrote that he did this in the name of broadmindedness, but this declaration is in itself an expedient of persuasive rhetoric. In his dialogues, thirty-four in all, Plato acknowledges numerous important philosophers by giving them a voice to speak out, but in his way. In the dialogues he exalts Socrates, who is nearly always the main protagonist, and he puts forward arguments against the Sophists by attributing to them extreme and depreciable statements. He was the first to make deliberate use of the "rhetorical dialogue" as a persuasive literary expedient (Boorstin, 1983). In his most mature and enriched dialogues, he explicitly presents and defends the strengths of his own thoughts. Plato used a series of "minor" dialogues to clear the ground of all the earlier theses, while indirectly suggesting something that he would only later present and demonstrate in an explicit way. In other words, Plato used his dialogues to bring forth declarations, in the persons of numerous thinkers who had preceded him, including Protagoras, Gorge, and Socrates, which were in reality his. Such work so greatly influenced the theories that followed that it led Whitehead (1947) to declare that "All the philosophy throughout nearly twenty centuries has been nothing but a series of footnotes on Plato's affirmations". Therefore, the first great "impostor of written thought" has determined nearly two thousand years of philosophy thanks to his explanatory ability based on the use of the communicative stratagem of the dialogue.

In the *Menone*, Plato formulates the *theory of reminiscence* for the first time. In this famous Socratic dialogue, Plato cleverly used a series of appropriate questions to get a geometry-naïve servant to demonstrate the Pythagorean Theorem of his own accord. Now Plato maintained that this was possible by virtue of the fact that man contains within him "reminiscent" knowledge that the philosopher can bring out by using his Maieutic art. He did not see it as due to the wise use of language that can persuade anyone of any belief, as declared by the Sophists. Therefore, knowledge itself once more regained an absolute value and ceased to be relative to man and to the arbiter. In Platonism, it is no longer man who measures the truth, as desired by Protagoras and the Sophists. Nor is it man who exposes the truth through reasoning, as shown by Socrates; but it is the metaphysical truth, the "absolute idea" that "measures" man and supplies him with the rules of thinking and of living. It seems evident that Plato betrayed his own master and his master's search to be free from dogmas, and introduced his own *absolutist* ideology (things-are-as-they-are).

Interestingly, when proposing ways to impose "absolute ideas", Plato does not refute the Sophists' rhetoric: rather he makes use of it, by stating that a clear and perfect discourse is determined by four aspects: what is needed to be said; how much needs to be said, taking into consideration the addressee and the time necessary to do so; what needs to be said should seem useful to whoever is listening; what should be said should neither be more nor less than what is sufficient in order to be understood. One should take into serious consideration the addressee, and regarding time, it is necessary that one speaks in the right moment, neither before nor after. Otherwise one will not speak well and will encounter failure (cited in Roncoroni, 1993).

It seems that in order to demonstrate the truth one should not be so tied to the truth.

The great majority of us were introduced to the sublime and ethereal idea of platonic love; however, Plato was not an exemplar of his own ideal—his loves were anything but platonic. Nevertheless, he still managed to portray this image of himself. It is the form through which something is presented, be it true or false, that renders it true. The efficient persuasion of the platonic dialogues is the most disarming example of this precept.

Thanks to all of this, Plato has managed, through the use of his explanatory art, to present to humanity something totally his own as something universal.

His dialectic consisted in moving from one sentence to another, from one concept to another, to the most general form of truth, to principles, to "ideas", until reaching metaphysics. This is why various religious people, believers in the most absolute truth (i.e., God), have always appreciated this philosopher. In fact, he was the one who first introduced the idea of *absolute truth* in the history of philosophy. Philosophy and faith are joined. Plato proposed in the *Republic* that those who do not conform to the truth should be locked up in rehabilitation centres, away from the citizenry. There, they should be re-educated until they come to accept the truth. Only then they can be brought back and integrated into the city.

In one of his *Unpopular Essays* (1950), Bertrand Russell very critically condemns the everlasting political "admiration" of Plato's work as a true "scandal". But the author underestimates the persuasive impact of the essays of this great philosopher in his examination, where, besides the technique of the dialogue, one can also find a sort of manual of the influencing ideology. This is why, by means of writing, Plato came to be considered as the master of persuasive philosophy. In fact, it was thanks to the success of Plato's work that the literary artefact of the dialogue became the rhetorical stratagem of the great Greek historians such as Plutarch, Herodotus, and Lucian (Boorstin, 1983).

In the wake of this, Aristotle, Plato's pupil, developed a dialectic based on the logic of "true–false" and "the excluded middle". From then on the persuasive rhetoric of both logic and science became relegated to a mere process of explanation by means of syllogisms or, better, by means of rigidly reductive, deductive processes. For example: "If something is white, it is not black", or else "All dogs have four limbs, so if something has four limbs it is a dog . . .".

But even in such cases, the reader becomes decidedly ambivalent in reading *The Rhetoric to Alexander*. In this book, which starts off with the most inquisitive accusations made against the Sophists, whom he defines as dishonest liars in his *Sophistic Refutations*, Aristotle proposes to his prince a series of communication techniques, decisively "Sophistic"; for example, "if you need to persuade somebody, use his own arguments".

One has to jump ahead to the founding of the Catholic church and its first medieval university to find another excellent example of the use of the dialogue as a form of persuasive rhetoric, in both texts and verbal disputes. In fact, the dialogue, the debate, and the discussion of theses through their oppositions and their alternatives are the bases of the search for knowledge and the truth of the "Scholastic Philosophy": medieval Christian philosophy.

Consequently, numerous rhetorical strategies were developed to successfully uphold intellectual arguments; structured in this way the dialogue became the instrument that brought man to accept the "truth" revealed in sacred writings. In this way the "religious dialogue" flourished: in verbal disputes between theologians about the church dogma and in the writing of ecclesiastical treatises. In addition to this, we find the literary form of dilemmas to be solved; the *insolubilia* dialogues between God and the devil. In the dialogue between the demonic figure that is always evil, that manipulates underhandedly, and the figure of God, that is always magnanimous, the scholars propose "insoluble" dilemmas to arrive at the conclusion that there are two possibilities: both good and bad exist, which side are you on? What might come as a surprise is the persuasive game created by the scholars and its use in many of their dissertations: the *illusion of alternatives*, the alternative between good and bad. A specific dialogue that holds all the truth within its two possibilities, yet it implicitly proposes one choice: good.

However, even back then somebody had rebelled against the "absolute truth" and was led to this conclusion through learned reasoning. He did so by using the same weapon as his enemies: the paradoxical dialogue. He is anonymous, since he was branded a heretic for proposing the dilemma in which the devil nails his rival, God, with an unsolvable request: "if you are omnipotent, then create a boulder so big that not even you can lift it". If God cannot lift the boulder, then he is not omnipotent, but he if he cannot create it, then he is also not omnipotent. Even beyond this irreverent example, medieval scholars promoted a unique persuasive work through the use of dialogues comprising an illusion of alternatives. Furthermore, from their debates, the first university, the University of Paris, arose, with all the other universities in Europe following in its wake.

St Thomas Aquinas is probably the most brilliant interpreter of this tradition. He developed the scholastic art of rhetoric in a first-class manner. The proof of this is his incredible *Summa Theologica*, where he guides the reader through "questions that create answers" to follow an itinerary that enhanced the thesis of the Catholic church. Like a funambulist of argumentation, he did not propose dogma but rather "interrogatives" through a literary dialogue constructed to lead the reader to predetermined answers.

In the medieval period, the "scientific dialogue" was developed in parallel with the religious dialogue. Therefore, even the virtually neutral field of science required and made use of a persuasive rhetoric to make the newly discovered thesis known and accepted by the common public.

Galileo Galilei understood that scientific truth would not concern all men, the entire society, in both the present and the future. Unlike other scientists of his time who preferred not to challenge the ecclesiastical authority, he wrote coarse language in the Dialogue that went beyond the two dominant systems of the world: Ptolemaic and Copernican. And he did so without explicitly affirming which of the two he eventually preferred. In reality, the intentions of Galileo were to show the unsustainable nature of Aristotelian physics and the truth of Copernican cosmology. He proposed the existence of a true physical proof, the tide phenomenon, that supported the Copernican theory of rotating bodies and the revolution of the earth. He attempted to explain the tides as the result of the complex motions between the earth's daily rotation and its annual revolution around the sun (an explanation which is nowadays known to be erroneous). To do so, he made use of the expository expedient of a dialogue between three persons with diverse complementary characteristics: the scholar, the religious person, and the ignorant man.

Thanks to this dialogue, not only were his theories accepted but he was not condemned for heresy. Even in this case, the rhetorical device of the dialogue generated fame for Galileo's theory (which probably would otherwise have remained obscure) beyond that acquired by his other most innovative theories. In fact, Galileo wrote his "Dialogue" after his theories had been strongly contrasted (Boorstin, 1983). The Copernican supposition was presented as a mathematical hypothesis without an effectively valid conclusion.

Instead, it is interesting to note that, in the analysis of the history of philosophy, there was no other author besides Blaise Pascal that more valued the logical persuasive power of the technique of the *illusion of alternatives*. It was this power that became highly exploited by the Scholastics. It was not due to chance that, through an eminent argumentation known as "the bet", Pascal managed to awaken our consciences to the cult of God, which had gone astray in the wake of the "selling of indulgences".

> I will tell you that you will thereby gain in this life, and that, at each step you take on this road, you will see such great certainty of gain, so much nothingness in what you risk, that you will at last recognise that you have wagered for something certain and infinite, for which you have given nothing. [Pascal, 1995, p. 233]

He affirms that between believing and non-believing in the existence of God and the Catholic hereafter, it is by far more convenient to believe, because if the hereafter does not exist you would not have lost, but if you did not believe in God and the hereafter *did* exist, you would have lost. There is only gain if you behave as a believer: by praying, by kneeling down, by making the sign of the cross on your forehead with holy water, because in this way there is at least a possibility that God exists, not to mention the possible benefits given by faith itself. Through the use of apparently rational arguments, Pascal leads the reader to a rational decision to believe in the irrational (Elster, 1979; Nardone, 2003a).

Thanks to Pascal's example, we have further proof of the fact that the "truth" becomes true in virtue of one's ability to present it in an acceptable and convincing way. The Sophists' relativism and their fine persuasive technique, even though condemned, seem to have been kept constantly veiled in the history of human thought and of its evolution.

In fact, even in subsequent centuries, the majority of the great scientists have presented their work in a form of dialogue (Boorstin,

1993; Helman, 2001). The most important discoveries that have changed the history of humanity have been presented, from a rhetorical point of view, as a dialogue between imaginary people who discuss a subject matter or else as a subtle dialogue between the author and his reader. In both cases, the dialogue succeeds in explicating the theories of the author as some inevitable evolution of the argument. Even Einstein, when presenting his Theory of Relativity, made use of a subtle dialogic style with his reader, which resulted in his acquiring great popularity as well as academic success.

Since the dawn of psychotherapy, the dialogue has represented a fundamental technique, not only as a model for presenting one's arguments but, moreover, as a investigative technique of the psyche and human behaviour.

Even Freud (1933a) seems to have acknowledged the magical power of words. He underlined this in the dialogue between the analyst and his patient, maintaining that words are the instrument of knowledge and change. Along with Freud, we see the rise of the "psychoanalytic dialogue", which consisted of a particular setting: the couch, and the position of the analyst behind the patient . . . a scenography ideally suited to amplifying the power of such a particular form of the dialogue. The patient, lying down without looking at the interlocutor, who remains seated behind his back, gives free rein to his mental associations. The comment of the psychotherapist thus *triggers off* other associations, so-called "free associations", which are followed by more interpretations. The entire structure of the psychoanalytic dialogue is orientated to increasingly value Freud's theories of the unconscious and render it a doctrine, instilled by means of a rigidly ritualized dialogic itinerary.

The wave of psychoanalysis, with its focus on the internal dialogue that takes shape from its theory, has dominated the scene for many years, and, even today, large numbers of followers declare its absolute "truth".

All of this has shifted attention from the *observable* to the *hidden*, from the interaction with others to one's own unconscious dynamics, founding, thus, by means of a specific rhetoric, a sort of platonic tyranny of the unconscious over the conscious: the psychoanalytic dialogue.

However, even before Freud, certain thinkers such as Bacon, Locke, and James had highlighted the enormous potential present in the communicative exchange between persons; the dialogue is considered as an instrument of knowledge and change in the individual and in his options. In particular, William James (1890, in Miller, 1983), who focused his research on personal and interpersonal processes, gave rise to a prolific tradition of systemic studies of language and communicative interaction, known as "Pragmatism".

George Mead (1966) followed the same path by analysing in more depth the symbolic interactions present in the dialogue between persons. Goffman (1969) then further developed this perspective and studied the dynamics of strategic interaction in-depth in order to better understand how individuals can consciously use dialogic techniques to help them reach their persuasive objectives.

There are two scholars that have effectively developed a rival project to the psychoanalytic doctrine: Milton Erickson and Carl Rogers. Erickson conducted his empirical and applied study on hypnosis and hypnotic language, and was responsible for the first formulation of the strategic approach in psychotherapy (Erickson, Rossi, & Rossi, 1979) and the systemization of suggestive communication techniques within a therapeutic dialogue. Rogers (1951) is renowned for the formulation of a model of clinical conversation meant to develop empathy, based on the "mirroring" technique, i.e., mirroring the client's behaviour. But it was not until the 1940s that one was able to witness a true recovery of, and a specific focus on, human science in communication and in the technique of the dialogue as an effective instrument to generate predetermined changes in the attitudes and behaviour of people. This means that 2400 years had to go by before seeing once more a systemic interest, free of dogmatic assumptions, in how the strategic use of language can induce radical change in the way people perceive and manage their reality. For this we have to thank Gregory Bateson and his famous group of scholars, who carried out the first research project on communication and its semantic, syntactic, and, most of all, pragmatic effect. By using video-recordings, Bateson, for the first time, systematically studied the different types of Sophistic techniques, such as antilogy, paradox, non-linear and non-ordinary logic. Bateson experimented on communication as an efficient instrument, suitable in all the human situations where rational logic and explanatory language fail, as, for example, in the case of severe psychotic disorders or in highly conflicting relationships.

It was not by chance that Bateson structured one of his most important works on a dialogue. In this dialogue, he uses questions posed by a young man and answers given by a sage as a device to firmly increase the efficiency of the contents and their expressive form for the reader. He coins the term *metalogo* to define a particular form of exposition, i.e., a combination of almost cryptic sentences and illuminating explanations.

Knowing through changing: the strategic dialogue

Hold clear in mind what you want to say, words will come along (Cato, in Astin, 1978).

"One just can't not communicate", is the first postulate of the pragmatics of communication (Watzlawick, 1977). Therefore, one has to choose whether to do so in a casual manner and undergo such inevitability, or choose to do so in a strategic manner that can be kept under control.

From this assumption stems the constructivistic and interactional strategic approach; that is, the application of theoretical and practical formulations to interpersonal and therapeutic communication developed from the work of the Palo Alto group (Nardone & Watzlawick, 1990; Watzlawick & Nardone, 1997; Watzlawick & Weakland, 1977). Rather than being based on an *a priori* theory of human nature where behaviour is "analysed", the constructivistic–strategic therapy model deals with the mode by which humans perceive and react to their own reality. The interactional–strategic therapists seek to understand a problem by examining a person's specific mode of communicating with himself, others, and the world, and transforming it from a dysfunctional to a functional one on which one can "operate". From such a perspective, human problems are seen merely as the products of the interaction between the subject and reality; thus, going back to the origin of the problem often leads one astray when searching for solutions.

For this reason, the work of the interactional–strategic therapist is *not* focused on why a problem exists but on how it functions, and especially on what to do to solve it, by guiding the person to change not only his/her behaviour but also his/her perceptive modality and causal attribution. All this takes place, mainly, through the dialogue between the therapist and the patient, where the former guides the latter to discover the mode by which his problems may be solved by making him perceive the situation from different perspectives to the pathological one.

The fundamental operative construct of this approach is the "attempted solution", formulated for the first time by the group of researchers at MRI (Mental Research Institute) in Palo Alto (Watzlawick, Weakland, & Fisch, 1974; Weakland, Fisch, Watzlawick, & Bordin, 1974). The attempted solutions are the reactions and behaviours of a person who is confronting difficulties in relationship with him/herself, others, and the world; these reactions and behaviours *complicate* rather than solve the problem and end up becoming rigid, redundant, dysfunctional models of interaction with reality. The dysfunctional behaviour therefore becomes the preferred reaction that one avails oneself of in a specific situation, and thus the problem is maintained because of what has been done in the attempt to solve it.

In order to substitute the dysfunctional attempted solution with a functional solution, it is necessary to study the mental, emotional, and relational "traps" in which people might find themselves. At the same time, it is necessary to identify the strategic levers of change, to get to know a problem through its solution (Nardone, 1993). As the aesthetic imperative of the famous cyberneticist Heinz von Foerster (1993) echoes, "if you want to see, learn to act".

This apparently simple construct is the basis for the evolution of the brief strategic therapy model of the Centre of Strategic Therapy (CTS) in Arezzo, which developed ever more efficient and effective therapeutic techniques. The CTS put together specific treatment protocols for particular pathologies such as obsessive disorders, phobic disorders, and eating disorders (Loriedo, Nardone, Watzlawick, & Zeig, 2002; Nardone, 1993, 2003a; Nardone & Cagnoni, 2002; Nardone & Watzlawick, 1990; Nardone, Verbitz, & Milanese, 2004; Watzlawick & Nardone, 1997). The CTS then expanded this knowledge into specific formulations to use in particular contexts, such as organizations, educational settings, and management (Nardone & Fiorenza, 1995; Nardone, Giannotti, & Rocchi, 2001; Nardone, Milanese, & Fiorenza, 2000).

We believe that the reader has recognized by now how this idea might collide with the traditional concept of psychotherapy based on the presupposition that to change a problematic behaviour one should primarily change the person's way of thinking. On the basis of this premise, the various forms of psychotherapies, cognitive, behavioural, or psychoanalytic, aim to achieve a change of *consciousness* in their patients in a way coherent with the respective theoretical assumptions; this implies the use of reasoning and indicative, descriptive, explanatory, confrontational, and interpretative language.

On the other hand, from a strategic perspective, change is prior to all actions and the therapeutic communication becomes its vehicle, or, better, does things with words (Austin, 1962).

Injunctions, suggestions, communicative artefacts and stratagems, and the rhetoric of persuasion are the principal vehicles of change in strategic therapy, since these sidestep the representation system of the person, and in this way they construct, without immediate awareness, alternative perceptions, actions, and cognitions.

Each session is like a chess game between the therapist and the patient, with successive moves meant to produce specific effects. After each change or result is achieved, one proceeds to redefine the change that took place and the ever-evolving situation. The therapeutic programme develops more and more tactics on the bases of the agreed objectives, and is continuously re-orientated to the observed effects.

"Knowing through changing" (Nardone & Portelli, 2005) therefore becomes the operative construct of the strategic intervention, because it is through changing the sensations and the vision of a person that we can lead him to discover new, solution-orientated ways of perceiving and managing his problems and difficulties.

Following this logic and the empirical and experimental research carried out, we have successfully designed specific treatment models for different pathologies and applied them to thousands of cases over a fifteen-year period (Nardone & Watzlawick, 2005). These specific protocols are composed of a sequence of therapeutic manoeuvres tailored *ad hoc* to the various forms of pathological persistence paired with the selection of specific stratagems to produce efficient and rapid therapeutic changes.

From the very beginning of our clinical research, communication and language have been the primary means through which particular therapeutic stratagems were applied. Thus, therapeutic communication has always undergone experimentation and elaboration. During recent years, referring back to the past activities carried out, we have focused on the evolution of therapeutic communication within our model, with the idea of developing ever more advanced techniques.

Looking back into the past has made us realize what awaits us in the future. In fact, we became aware that, over time, the first session dialogue has undergone such a thorough evolution that it has become a strategy composed of a set of stratagems that makes the patient active in finding a solution to his problems from the very start of the encounter.

Once more, *non-ordinary* logic has come to our rescue and has turned our looking into the past into a means by which we can look ahead to the future. Thanks to more efficient, efficacious, and rigorous therapeutic strategies, we have conjugated an even more strategic form of dialogue.

Such an evolution of therapeutic communication has led the first session to become not only a diagnostic and preliminary phase prior to the intervention, but rather a true therapeutic strategy in itself. With the strategic dialogue, the investigation transformed itself into a true intervention.

The questions, rather than guiding only the therapist to understand the persistence of the problem to be solved, became the vehicle by which the patient is led to "feel" things differently. In this way, the therapist uses the dialogue to induce the patient's reactions to change and bring to light his resources that have been jammed by the previously held rigid and pathological perceptions.

In the wake of this, the style of conducting the first session has been completely modified, starting with the formulation of the investigation of the problem to be solved. The questions have been altered in their interrogative form and are no longer open-ended, such as: "When you have a panic attack what do you feel?", but have become closed, holding a sort of illusion of alternatives: "When you have a panic attack, do you fear dying or losing control?" This makes the person reply by taking up one of the planned answers.

Obviously, this question is only possible because of ten years of experience in studying panic attacks in all their forms and getting to know them through their solutions. This helped us understand that those who suffered from this type of pathology have a series of redundancies that repeat themselves, including either the fear of dying or of losing control. This not only applies to this type of pathology, but to all types of pathologies.

This is not reformulating a new type of diagnostic model; on the contrary, in this case we are "knowing through changing" and not "knowing (first) to then change".

The diagnostic procedure already becomes an intervention; better still, the most important of all interventions. In fact, if I had to say to a person suffering from panic attacks,

"When you have a panic attack do you fear losing control or dying?"

and the patient replies (like the majority of the cases seen in the last decade):

"I fear losing control,"

I have already reduced by half the possibilities.

The second question could be:

"Are you afraid of losing control in situations you can predict, or are these absolutely unpredictable?"

In the majority of the cases, the person replies,

"Well, I don't know! . . . but if I had to stop and think for a while, I might say this happens in certain situations."

Thus we reply,

"And can you predict these situations?"

The patient replies,

"Well yes, now that you've made me think about it, I can predict when this might happen. For example, when I have to go somewhere on my own ... or if I'm in a crowd ... or if I'm in a closed space ... or if I'm in elevated places ...",

depending on the type of phobia.

Just like a funnel that gets narrower and narrower, we are guided by the dialogue until we discover how the problem functions. But, since the therapist and patient make this discovery together, we define this dialogue as a *discovery reached by two*.

Along these lines, therapy becomes a discovery within which the patient and the therapist together learn how the problem functions through a series of questions and answers, and a series of strategic phrasing, and start introducing changes in the perception of the patient. But this process will surely become clearer to the reader as proceed in this exposition.

Let us now analyse what we have managed to obtain thanks to the two questions given above. We have already obtained quite a vast amount of information because now we know that the person does not fear dying, but rather losing control, and that this takes place in situations he can predict. But this is what the therapist has come to understand. The patient has begun to have a clearer map of his problem, complete with precise co-ordinates. He then starts wondering if, in reality, he does not fear dying, something that he might already know but that he has now put into focus, and whether all this takes place in predictable situations.

To proceed beyond this point, it is useful to take a step backwards that will allow us to leap two steps forward. With this intent, it is important to use a paraphrase that will help us confirm that we are moving in the right direction and that anchors the perception of the patient about the functioning of the problem in the new perspective.

Thus we can tell the person:

"Please correct me if I'm wrong [taking up a one-down submissive position] ... but you are telling me that you suffer from panic attacks and this corresponds to a fear of losing control, and that this takes place in a situation you can predict."

The patient will reply:

"Yes, I believe so!"

By expressing approval and agreement between the expert and the person asking for help, it seems as if we are moving along a multi-lane highway, and, through a sequence of manoeuvres, we progressively eliminate lateral lanes to end up with just one lane: the one that leads to change.

In doing so, we are only proceeding along a narrowing-down path of logic that leads to the solution, while we are at the same time acquiring something else, which is just as important. By declaring "Please, correct me if I'm wrong", we make the patient feel as if he is leading the discovery process of our dialogue. In such way, he will not feel disqualified, but rather gratified. The sensation is not of finding oneself either in front of a doctor that tells one "Do this, do that . . .", or in front of someone who tells one "You suffer from an illness called panic", thus one feels understood, emotionally reinforced, and acknowledged.

In this way, we establish an emotionally positive relationship that amplifies the collaboration and the subject's expectations of therapy. Furthermore, he will be more aware of how he can manage the problem and how it functions, and not on what might have caused the problem. The patient goes through this process with the illusion of leading it all. We believe that the reader by now has come to comprehend how we proceed in sowing the seeds of change in the patient through the use of such a dialogue, which seems to be structured in quite a simple way but which is, in fact, a complex and advanced method.

Proceeding with the strategic questioning, the third question suitable for this case is:

"When encountering such situations, do you tend to avoid or face the situation?"

By virtue of these questions we are able to determine whether the person tends to avoid because of his fear, or, rather, tends to give up only after facing the situation unsuccessfully. Either reply opens up a different scenario and requires diverse strategies in the evolution of the dialogue.

Imagine that the person replies,

"I tend to avoid the situations."

Then the following question should be:

"But if you can't really avoid it, what do you do: do you ask for help or do you face it on your own?",

and generally the person replies,

"Well, I ask for help."

This is a very important question since it determines whether the person is dependent on someone or whether he tries to make it on his own, and this will orientate us to a completely different evolution of the treatment. This is because, in the case of the former, we focus on breaking the dependency and bringing the person to recognize his resources, but in the latter, we base our intervention on dismantling the trap into which the person has drawn himself. Thanks to this answer, we have added another piece of strategic knowledge: the person either avoids threatening situations; or else asks for help in order to face them.

Now we can paraphrase once more to confirm and redefine:

"Correct me if I'm wrong . . . so you are a person who suffers panic attacks that might take place in situations you can predict, and thus you tend to avoid such situations. But if you can't possibly avoid them, you need somebody to accompany you who can act promptly in case you feel sick."

"That's it!"

replies the patient.

The reader should grant himself time to analyse the four questions, the induced answers, and the two paraphrases in their specific sequence as a form of therapeutic strategy.

Thanks to these manoeuvres we now hold a lot of operative information on how the problem functions. At the same time, even the patient's mind starts focusing on the functioning of his problem and how he usually tends to manage it; his dysfunctional attempted solutions are revealed with great clarity.

Moreover, the person feels understood, and simultaneously acknowledges that he is in front of a competent therapist because the latter is putting forward decidedly crucial questions. This will considerably increase the patient's therapeutic expectancy and will reinforce the relationship between the therapist and the patient.

Hubble, Duncan, and Miller (1999) declare that a strong therapeutic relationship is responsible for over 70% of the change generated in therapy. And if we add to this, as in our case, the opening up to new perspectives that make the patient feel that there is a possible solution, the therapeutic gradient is boosted even more.

Once this is achieved, we usually then put forward other successive strategic questions and reframing paraphrases:

"Do you tend to speak a lot about your problem or you keep everything to yourself?"

Let's imagine that the person replies:

"I speak about it with everyone."

From a strategic point of view, we have a much clearer picture. We have enough information to start the most active phase of change. In fact, we now have a clear idea about how the problem functions based on the three basic dysfunctional attempted solutions usually put into practice by the person suffering the panic attack. Now we can proceed to indirectly guide the patient towards change; it is as if we are launching a snowball, which rolls until it becomes an avalanche. With this objective in mind we then ask,

"And when you speak about it do you feel better or worse?"

And the patient replies,

"Well, I feel better because I feel relieved."

And thus we ask,

"You told us that when you speak about the problem, in that moment you feel better because you feel relieved. But after some time, do you feel better or you feel worse?"

Usually the person will look at you and reply,

"Now that you made me think, afterwards I feel very frustrated."

Thus the paraphrase that follows is:

"Therefore, if I'm not mistaken, you tend to speak a lot about your problem and when you disclose it, you feel better because you feel relieved but soon after you feel even more frustrated because you recognize your incapability once more."

And the person who is nailed down to perceive things through a new perspective, usually answers,

"Yes, that is true!"

We are starting to introduce change in his perceptions and emotions regarding his attempted solutions, which were first perceived as useful but which in the long run end up making the situation worse.

Following this pattern of introducing changes through evoking new sensations about the failed attempted solutions used by the subject, we proceed with another question:

"And when you ask for help in order to be able to face a threatening situation, and this person helps you, do you feel better or worse?"

Usually the person replies,

"Better! Yes. However, afterwards . . . I feel worse because I always feel more incapable."

"Ah! So, please correct me if I'm wrong, but when you ask for help and you receive it, at that very moment you feel better because you feel safe, but soon after you feel even more incapable, because when you receive help from others, this proves the fact even more that you cannot make it on your own, and this makes you feel worse . . ."

And the person once more replies,

"Yes, that is true!"

Once more we are introducing change through a series of questions and paraphrases that make the person *feel* rather than *understand*. He then feels that when he speaks about his problem or asks for help, it worsens the situation; thus, this renders fear no longer a limit but a resource. In fact, a bigger fear, i.e., that of worsening the situation, will kill the smaller fear, i.e., that which makes him ask for help.

From our point of view, it is a decisively important difference between "feeling" and "understanding", because there is a dated misconception regarding people: "they need to understand something in order to change it" even though we are faced every day with proof that this is not so. Every single one of us has, at sometime or another, felt the frustration of wanting to free ourselves from something but being unable to do so. For example, we understand well that we are sharing our life with the wrong person, so we would like to break free, but we feel that we are so attached to that person that we cannot take such a step. Is there a better proof that shows the difference between feeling and understanding?

From a strategic point of view, therapy should aim to make the person feel differently towards something and not understand it differently; to change the perception regarding something and not to change the cognition, because if the perception is changed then the emotional reaction will change, thus changing the behavioural reaction and, as a final effect, eventually changing the cognition. The great majority of psychotherapies work to change cognition, behaviour or emotions. But that which triggers off every process is what we feel, how we perceive, and all the rest follows.

Returning to our case, the patient is led to feel differently through the use of our questions and paraphrases. The patient begins to feel that every time he asks for and receives help, or every time he speaks about his problem and is heard, the situation gets worse, even though in that very moment he feels better. This allows us to ask something of him that would otherwise have been impossible to ask: to avoid asking for help and to avoid always speaking about it. The person can accept this now because first he felt the need to stop it and then understood that this could help him.

The patient went through a process of discovery together with the therapist. The patient perceives that he "conducted" the discovery because he was the one to give answers to the questions, so he feels induced and not forced. The therapist has only confirmed and paraphrased his answers and constructed the process though a series of focused questions.

In this way one can guide the patient to discover new perceptions that determine new reactions to the problem right from the first session. In so doing, we subtly introduce a chain reaction of changes: knowing through changing.

At this point in the session, we further reinforce the effects of what has already been reached. So we introduce a manoeuvre that evokes strong sensations to firmly impress the necessity and inevitability of change, something that was not even contemplated by the person until that moment.

> "Please allow me to recap all that which has been said and, if I'm not mistaken, otherwise please do correct me, you are a person who suffers from panic attacks that take place in situations you can predict, which you tend to avoid. But if you cannot avoid them, then you ask for help and speak quite a lot about it. And when you do so, you first feel relieved and feel better, but afterwards this makes you feel worse, because if others listen to you, this means that there is truly something wrong with you. The same applies to when you ask for help in order to face a situation you cannot avoid, and, thus, at the very moment having help from others makes you feel safe, but afterwards you feel even more incapable because if others need to help you, this means that you cannot make it on your own."

The person replies,

> "Yes, that is the way things are!"

> "Well, what we have said so far brought to my mind a phrase by a well-known poet, Fernando Pessoa, who wrote, 'you bear the wounds of the battles you never fought', and I would add—the wounds of evaded battles never truly heal."

Just like a branding iron, this aphorism makes a deep impression on the person. We regard the aphorism as the strongest literary form of communication, being highly and immediately evocative. It brings a person to feel something without explaining it, while entailing no great effort because it takes effect immediately and leaves the interlocutor bewildered, pupils dilated, looking just like a deer in the headlights. The aphorism will leave a mark inside his mind in the same way that a hot iron would mark the skin.

But what have we done so far? We introduced certain questions, paraphrases, and followed them with an aphorism. However, through doing seemingly little, we have really achieved a great deal, since we have introduced a very radical change in the patient's perception. This is because now the person holds a clearly felt perception that certain things he had been doing to protect himself from fear ended up maintaining the situation and even worsening it. We did not just "explain" that the attempted solutions worsen the problem as well as maintaining it, but we have made the person "feel" it. This is a "corrective emotional experience"; the vision of a new reality through a process of discovery, which the person thinks he has led. He has not been forced into it, and the reader knows well that "we are usually convinced more easily by reasons we have found ourselves than by those which have occurred to others", as affirmed by Blaise Pascal (*Pensées*, 1995), who, not by chance, is considered to be one of the greatest persuaders in history.

Therefore, through the therapeutic manoeuvres described above, the person discovers that his attempted solutions actually worsen his situation. In other words, the strategic dialogue creates a type of reframing by a process of discovery that my dear master–friend Paul Watzlawick would call a "casual planned event". Although the therapist has planned this event, the patient experiences it as a discovery that he has come to on his own, and so feels as if it were a spontaneous personal evolution. In this way resistance to change is nullified, because it is felt not as something imposed by external figures, but rather as a natural internal inclination, a result of the discovery that brought about this change in perspective.

Now the patient will be more open to accept suggestions to put direct prescriptions into practice, thanks to what has already taken place in the session. Thus, different behaviour modalities become a joint achievement of the therapist and the patient. Directivity turns into collaboration. To give an example of how the patient described in this case would be more willing to try a prescriptive practice, we might say to him:

"Very well! From now until the next time we meet, I would like you to think about what we have discussed today together: that is, every time you speak about the problem you make it worse. I would like you to think that every time you ask for help and you receive it, you make things worse, even though at that very moment you feel better. The same goes for when you avoid something, because, just like Pessoa, you will be bearing the wounds of the evaded battles. But I cannot ask you to stop doing this, because you are not yet ready . . ."

This is a prescriptive stratagem: first we evoke the fear of something and then declare a small paradoxical provocation, "however, you are not ready to do so . . ." after having put a bigger fear, that of getting worse, against the fear itself.

"Therefore I cannot ask you to stop avoiding or to stop asking for help because you are not yet capable . . . however, every time you're about to do so think that this will not only maintain the problem but make it worse. However, I can ask you to avoid speaking about it because this is easier . . ."

This communicational manoeuvre reinforces the effect of the previous reframe and indirectly curbs the "socializing" carried out about the problem; an indication proposed as being easy to carry out in contrast to the other two, which are declared to be almost impossible for the person. The reader will surely recognize this to be a variant of the illusion of alternatives technique.

Then we proceed to administer the only direct prescription, which you can see is actually another therapeutic stratagem.

"... I have prepared a simple table for you with various columns, which you should copy into a portable notebook that you should carry with you wherever you go, just like a true captain's logbook. From now until the next time we meet, every time you feel sick, you feel one of those critical moments coming on . . . just at that very moment, wherever you are and with whomever you are, bring out the notebook and write in it. However, it is important that you do so at the very moment this happens to you, not before, otherwise you will tell me your fantasy, nor afterwards, because you will be telling me a memory. I need you to give me a sort of instant photo of the problem. This will help me understand how your problem functions exactly and will help me to identify which are the strategies specific for you."

Thus, we give the logbook table to the patient, which seems like a diagnostic monitoring of the panic episodes but is, in reality, a technique useful for shifting attention away from the symptom. In the art of stratagems it is the first stratagem: "ploughing the sea unknown to the skies". By writing the log, the patient's attention is diverted from listening to himself carrying out the given task. Thus, what might appear to be a further focus on the symptom serves in reality to make it dissipate.

Usually, patients come back to the second session reporting no episodes of panic attack or, if they did experience one, they notice that annotating interrupted its escalation. But the most interesting aspect is usually that they typically cease speaking about the problem and asking for help, because they are afraid of making things worse. For a person who suffers from panic attacks, finding himself able to confront previously avoided situations on his own after such a long time makes him discover certain resources that he previously thought he did not possess. There is nothing as enthusing for someone who had been blocked by fear for such a long time as discovering that he can do things without being afraid, and that the reality that previously terrorized him now no longer does. On the contrary, such people discover that they can confront those situations tranquilly.

Just like almost all complex things, the strategic dialogue, in order to be efficacious, needs to be rendered by the therapist and perceived by the interlocutor as a simple and natural process.

By leading the first session this way over the past four years, we found that 69–70% of patients had their symptoms reduced to zero between the first and the second session. These results are reflective of the majority of the psychopathologies treated with this method.

The example put forward is only one of the various possible applications of this innovative technique. In fact, during past years, laborious empirical research has produced a series of strategic questions and specific paraphrases for many types of pathology with similar results to those presented here. However, it is important to note that the strategic dialogue is not a rigidly structured interview, since it can be continuously corrected by the patient's confirmations or disconfirmations of the therapist's paraphrases made every two or three questions. Therefore it is a *self-corrective* discovery. One can correct an error before actually making it, or before creating irreparable trouble. This might be of great help, both for the patient, who avoids risk, and for the therapist, who constantly holds a measure of his/her doings.

Just as when one is faced with the dilemma of identifying a random square chosen on a chessboard (an example often presented in our books), one can reduce the possibilities from sixty-four squares to two by means of only six strategic questions, and then arrive at the solution. This takes place because every strategic question reduces significantly the field under investigation while opening up new sceneries of change.

Let us consider a chessboard, which, as the reader might know, is made up of sixty-four squares, alternating black and white (Figure 1).

The challenge is to guess which of the sixty-four squares I've chosen.

As one can well understand, finding the right answer might seem rather complicated. But, if we use a strategic perspective, a non-ordinary logic of problem solving, and tailor this to the problem and the objective to be reached, we can proceed in this way.

We should first ask the interlocutor if the chosen square is in the right or the left half of the chessboard. After such a question we would have halved the possibilities. Then we should ask if the chosen square is in the upper or lower half of the selected part, and in this way we reduce the possibilities to a quarter. We should then ask if the chosen square is in the left or right half of the remaining part of the chessboard, and in this way we would end up with only eight possibilities left. Regarding the remaining part, we should

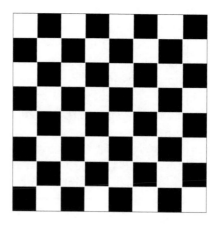

Figure 1. A chessboard.

then ask if the chosen square is in the upper or lower half, and thus four possibilities will remain. Then we should ask once more if the chosen square is in the left or right half of the chessboard and come to only two possibilities. Thus, we can now ask whether the chosen square is the upper one or the lower.

The result will be that the right answer is acquired through just six questions (see Figure 2, a–e), because we have used a logical stratagem that subsequently appears exceedingly simple and that reminds us of the famous Italian expression "Uovo di Colombo" ("The Egg of Columbus").[1]

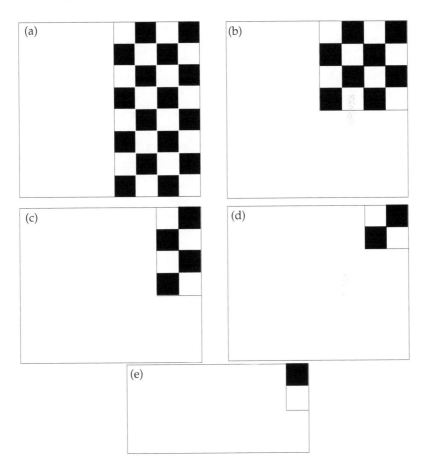

Figure 2. The consecutive results of the questioning process.

As Wittgenstein (1980) said, "Every explanation is a hypothesis". Our hypothetical explanation of this powerful, yet subtle and apparently simple instrument is that one can work simultaneously on various levels, as Saulo Sirigatti (1999), an illustrious scholar of psychology, suggests in a personal communication. We work on the patient's perception of the problem. We work on the emotional relationship with the therapist. And we work on his/her expectations to combine all the successive effects without making the patient feel manipulated, because it is s/he who is guiding and s/he who is giving the answers. At the same time, change takes place in his/her behaviour, his/her attempted solutions.

We therefore work simultaneously on the perceptive, emotive, and behavioural level. As a final effect, change takes place even on a cognitive level, but only once the pathology has been unblocked.

From this case the reader can see how we invert the usual process of all psychotherapies because first we obtain change and then awareness follows, while in the majority of therapies one looks first for awareness in order to produce change.

It is clear that this therapy is indebted to the *Art of Stratagems* (Nardone, 2003b) since even this process is in reality a strategy. In the words of Lao Tzu (cited in Hendricks, 1989): "Flexibility triumphs over rigidity, weakness over force. All that is malleable is always superior to all that is immobile. This is the principle according to which control over things is attainable in collaboration to the supremacy of adaptability."

Notes

1. The expression "The Egg of Columbus" is equivalent to the English expression "as plain as the nose on your face", or the American "thinking outside the box". The story narrates that a courtier of shallow wit, with the purpose of throwing discredit on the achievement of Columbus, intimated that it was not so great an exploit after all; all that was necessary was to sail west a certain number of days; the lands lay there waiting to be discovered. Were there not other men in Spain, he asked, capable of this?

    The response of Columbus was to take an egg and ask those present to make it stand upright on its end. After they had tried and tried, but failed, he struck the egg on the table and, by cracking the shell, he gave it a base on which to stand.

"But anybody could do that!" cried the critic.

"Yes; and anybody can become a discoverer when once he has been shown the way," retorted Columbus. "It is easy to follow in a known track."

CHAPTER TWO

The structure of the strategic dialogue

"A lot of words are never evidence of elevated wisdom"

(Talete)

Questions with an illusion of alternatives

"The great majority of the problems do not derive from the given answers but from the questions we put forward." With this sentence we refer to Immanuel Kant's work, *Critique of Practical Reason* (1997), or, better, the idea that questions create answers rather than thesis inducing questions. From this perspective, the well-known philosopher and a great part of modern epistemology have put forward scientific methods with which to construct correct questions. One just needs to recall Einstein's teachings: "It is our theory that determines our observations".

However, though such a rationalistic approach has demonstrated the fundamental importance of the interdependency between questions and answers in the scientific, empirical--experimental, and hypothesis formulation/verification fields, it has dealt very little with the suggestive, evocative, and persuasive effects of the dialogue. In other words, rigorous scientific analysis has forgotten all about *rhetoric*; underestimating the weight this has had even in the history of science.

In fact, all great scientists have made use of rhetoric (as previously described) to have their innovative theories accepted and to overcome their colleagues' obstinate resistance to change (Nardone & Domenella, 1994).

The persuasive power of putting forward questions that create answers is an art known from antiquity: Protagoras was the first great proponent to systemize it, and he defined it as the "Eristic art". This was made up of a process of questions that led the interlocutor to give answers that contradicted his previous assumptions, thus leading him to change his perspective through a personal discovery. Therefore, Protagoras never wrestled against the thesis of his interlocutor by proposing his own, but acted in a way to bring his interlocutor to renounce his own, through personal intuition. Back in the seventeenth century, Pascal (1995) had also affirmed that self-persuasion is better and more efficient.

The Eristic Art of Protagoras is the most ancient persuasive technique, structured in the form of "strategic dialogue".

This Sophist tradition is the foundation of the modern strategic approach, developed through the experience of, and experimentation with, the model as therapeutic communication with thousands of clinical cases and a dozen managerial cases over a period of ten years (Nardone, Milanese, Mariotti, & Fiorenza, 1999; Watzlawick & Nardone, 1997).

In fact, over the years, there have been numerous thinkers, philosophers, scientists, and artists who pursued the art of the dialogue as a form of persuasive exposition of their theses, but none proposed a rigorous codification.

The nineteenth century witnessed the publication of the first mini-manuals regarding the art of communication, but these indicated the modality of *affirmation* rather than of *questioning*. Thus, throughout the twentieth century, reference to the rhetoric of individual or mass persuasion was solely and constantly focused on the techniques that lead to manipulation through highly injunctive language.

Therefore, the art of proposing questions that open up new scenarios has only continued to be an effective instrument through inventions and creative practices (Altshuller, 2000), where it is necessary to find new solutions to unsolved problems. Here, inventors and other creative people have always pursued and studied the stratagem of proposing questions to differentiate and elaborate diverse perspectives of reality that elaborate themselves in a spiral form.

William James (1890) affirmed that genius is nothing other than "the ability to perceive things from an non-ordinary perspective". In this light, one can imagine how an inventor reaches innovative discoveries by asking himself particular questions based on his non-ordinary perspective. In the same way, each one of us can discover new solutions to our problems by undergoing particular forms of questioning.

This means that, just like an inventor, one might discover new and efficient solutions that were previously invisible by formulating and trying to respond to questions that lead one to assume diverse perspectives about the problem.

By doing so we are able to influence our interlocutor in a subtle way, rather than trying to force our point of view on to him or her (Loriedo, 2001).

A person is spontaneously led to different territories totally new to them by trying to respond to the strategic questions, which are designed to create "alternatives" that guide one towards persuasional objectives.

Descartes (1637) teaches that each one of us should make his or her own discoveries "because nobody can understand well enough and truly own something if learnt from somebody, in contrast to when one learns it on his own".

However, the most extraordinary example of the persuasive power of advancing sequential strategic questions to lead someone to spontaneously persuade himself through his own answers is without any doubt the *Summa Teologica* of Thomas Aquinas (1920). In this masterpiece, St Thomas interlocutes with his reader by putting forward more than hundred questions, thus leading the reader towards certain specifically desired answers. For example: "Is the sacred doctrine a Science?" Questions were followed by objections and then their rebuttal. He engaged in a rigorous dialogic process that started with God and passed through the order of creation until it arrived at the complex of the Christian doctrine. It was made up of aimed questions and answers in the form of a scholastic dispute that arrives at the most "corrective and rigorous" answers: or, rather, the already preset objective of the dissertation. Just as a strategic sage of Ancient China would affirm, the reader is led up to the attic and then the ladder is removed.

The extraordinary power of persuasion as such an influencing process resides in the fact that it seems the very opposite. It does not prescribe, but induces one to new perspectives that the subject feels they have discovered on their own and not as the result of an injunction imposed by others.

The shift is from direct manipulation to an indirect induction of strategic self-deceptions. But, if we employ suggestive techniques in addition to the persuasive power of argumentation given by the questions, the effect will be even more amazing. In our case, since our objective is to lead the patient out of his mental trap, the questions become true therapeutic instruments if they are well constructed and adequately suggestive. They induce in the subject, who is entrapped in his pathological perceptions and reactions, new modalities of feeling and reacting to his realities.

In other words, the strategic questions allow the patient to substitute her dysfunctional self-deceptions with functional ones, because she will transform the way she manages and perceives things, having been induced by her own replies.

In order to make this therapeutic instrument ever more efficient, we have turned to a well-known suggestive communication technique: the *illusion of alternatives*.

This technique represents one of the most elegant forms of injunction (Loriedo, 2001; Nardone & Watzlawick, 1990; Watzlawick, 1980), that is described by Erickson, Rossi, and Rossi (1979) as an efficient communication instrument to arrive at therapeutic prescriptions, to be applied in cases where one expects resistance from the patient in following the therapist's indications.

However, in the case of the strategic dialogue, the illusion of alternatives is used not to prescribe actions, but rather to induce answers to the strategic questions. In other words, the question is the structure that offers the interlocutor two opposing possibilities, and he can decide which of the two best fits his situation. The art of persuasion proceeds with a series of these questions, which funnel the subject to a turning point about his previous assertions using his own given answers. All this is carried out in a way that leads the subject to feel the need for change, prompted by the newly discovered and substituting perceptions acquired throughout the dialogue.

Thus, the strategic dialogue with the illusion of alternatives starts with more generalized questions, then narrows down in a spiral fashion and builds upon answers that reveal potentially critical aspects of the particular emerging situation. As François Jullien (1996) points out in his *Treaty of Efficiency*, it is all about evoking the action potential of a situation through a condition constructed *ad hoc* to mobilize its resources.

This means that the sequence, like the questions themselves, is not rigid and pre-established but, rather, adapted and tailored to the logic of the interlocutor, just like a custom-made suit.

In fact, on the bases of such logic and its correlates, specific questions and their proposed alternative answers are constructed to call the perception of the subject into question on something and to reorientate it towards more functional directions.

The process is a sort of an interactive "dance" between questions that create answers and answers that allow the construction of the successive strategic questions. This continues until the interlocutor declares that he changed his position following the new assumed perceptions yielded by the discoveries acquired through the dialogue.

It is necessary to clarify that, in order for illusion of alternatives questions to be real therapeutic instruments and vehicles of change, they need to be focused on the perceptions and reactions of the subject about her particular problem. They should focus on the concrete interaction between the person and her problematic reality, on her failed attempts to manage it, and on the vision that is feeding it. Pythagoras, 2500 years ago, had already warned, "bear in mind that humans are themselves instigators of their own misfortunes" (Roncoroni, 2003).

Consequently, the questions propose a pair of opposing reactions to the problem as alternatives; for example:

1. "Do you think that your problem is unique and unrepeatable or is part of an array of problems?"
2. "When faced by problematic situations, do you tend to run away or confront them directly?"

3.   "Do you confront your problem on your own or do you ask for help?"

The alternative answers refer to the subject's possible perceptions of the problem and the modalities used to fight it, thus offering her an operative image of how she constructs what she eventually endures.

In other words, the process of strategic questioning follows a funnel-like sequence, leads the interlocutor to discover ways that he is the instigator of his destiny, and thus shows how his dysfunctional attempted solutions, based on those erroneous perceptions, feed the problem. This process of induced discovery produces a real perceptual *saltus* (leap) in the subject (Thom, 1989) because it short-circuits the perceptive and reactive vicious circle, proving how dysfunctional and dangerous it is.

This change in perspective has an emotional impact comparable to an *enlightenment*, using Buddhist terms. People usually react with total astonishment when they discover that what they have thought and did so far in order to defeat the problem actually helped to maintain it.

This represents a true and proper "emotionally corrective experience", which makes the subject undergo change in her previous mental and behavioural scripts. Thus, the successive indications for the concrete realization of change would find a wide-open path free of resistance. It may now be clearer to the reader how the technique of strategic questioning with an illusion of alternatives is orientated to scan and funnel the rigidly pathological perceptions of the patient and the consequent behavioural reactions. These questions guide the patient towards change by making her acquire more elastic and efficient ways of interacting with her problems. There is a movement from unworkable solutions that feed the problem to functional solutions that break it. However, such a substitution is not suggested or prescribed, but is arrived at through a course of questioning that leads the patient to discover that which solves the problem soon after revealing that which maintains it.

This is the reason why the achieved change is not a superficial modelling or an attempt to control the reactions of the subject, but is a radical alteration of his perceptions and causal attributions. From this follows an even better revelation of the real efficiency of the method, because it does not merely change the actions but also the perceptions that induce them, or, rather, it completely changes the interaction between the subject and his reality. Marcel Proust (1981) stated, "the true journey of discovery is not to see new worlds but to change one's eyes".

The reframing paraphrases

"Words differently arranged have different meanings and meanings differently arranged have different effects" (*Pensées* I: 23). This affirmation of Blaise Pascal's (1995) is a clear evocation of the theme of this section.

The second component of the strategic dialogue, which is interdependent with the questions with an illusion of alternatives, is the *reframing paraphrases*.

With this definition we refer to a manoeuvre that follows every two or three questions, uses the answers given to formulate a vision of the problem, and verifies its correct comprehension to the interlocutor.

This means that no evaluation or interpretation is directly proposed, but, in a way that makes no assumptions, a verification is carried out regarding the subject's comprehension of the function of the problem. For example:

> " Correct me if I'm wrong, from what you have affirmed it seems that ...?"

Therefore the specialist steps aside from the role of the expert and verifies his/her formulations about the presenting problem with the patient. In so doing, the specialist inverts the usual interaction between expert and the person asking for help. It appears that it is the latter who guides the conversation and is the true expert on the problem, since it is his/hers.

Paraphrasing the answers given to the previous two or three strategic questions will make the subject feel respected, not forced into something and not feeling disqualified because the expert he referred to asks for confirmation of his/her valuation rather than just declaring it.

This creates a collaborative atmosphere and relationship between the two, which will help to circumvent possible resistance and misunderstanding and which also represents a true therapeutic component of the dialogue. The person not only feels accepted but also holds the main role in the investigation of his/her own problem. Paraphrasing the answers to the questions brings the failed attempted solutions to light and reveals them as rather counterproductive in trying to manage the problem, inevitably reorientating the attention of the patient on the pathological vicious circle they are engaged in. Therefore, unlike other structured investigative forms, the strategic dialogue puts the patient in a position "to feel" the need to change what has increased, rather than reduced, the problem so far. Once more Pascal helps us to comprehend the process of persuasion when he affirms:

> When we wish to correct with advantage and to show another that he errs, we must notice from what side he views the matter, for on that side it is usually true, and admit that truth to him, but reveal to him the side on which it is false. He will be satisfied with that, for he sees that he was not mistaken and that he only failed to see all sides. Now, no one is offended for not seeing everything, but one does not like to be mistaken, and that perhaps arises from the fact that man naturally cannot see everything, and that naturally he cannot err in the side he looks at, since the perceptions of our senses are always true. [Pascal, 1995, I: 9]

In a subtle way, paraphrasing the answers given to the strategic questions opens the person up to new perspectives that had not been available to him until then because he was entrapped in his rigid perceptual scripts, and makes him discover how dysfunctional those scripts were. Such a concrete experience, this corrective discovery, induces an inevitable change in his reactions towards the problematic situation.

The request for confirmation of the expert's formulations, produced from the interlocutor's answers, is therefore not only a verification of the accuracy of the diagnosis, but also induces by itself a perceptual change in that something that had previously seemed helpful will be seen as dangerous from now on.

In fact, giving confirmations to the strategic therapist's investigation makes the patient feel as if she is a sort of travelling companion who lends a hand in order to avoid wrong turns in the course of getting to know her problem. But, unconsciously, she is shifting the paraphrasing that is being proposed to her in a way that activates a sort of self-persuasion. Replying to somebody who asks for a confirmation of one's assertions, "Yes . . . things are just the way you are saying . . .", not only gives a confirmation to the interlocutor but persuades oneself of the correctness of such vision. All this takes place as a sort of first-person discovery made by the patient, given by her answers to the questions proposed by the interlocutor, who apparently plays the "non-expert" since she sends them back rearranged together with a request for confirmation. If, on the contrary, the interlocutor is not in accord with the reframing paraphrase, this indicates that we are on the wrong track and that we need to adjust our course.

Therefore, the paraphrase can strategically induce change in the interlocutor or induce a change of direction in our investigation. In other words, it is either corrective for the person who is asking for help or for the person who is trying to help; this allows the latter to reorientate her explanations until she acquires assent for her paraphrases by the interlocutor.

Now, as the reader might well understand, the interdependency between the illusion of alternatives sequences, focused on the dysfunctional attempted solutions, and the paraphrases, focused overtly on confirming assertions and covertly on reframing perceptions and reactions to the problem, seems clearer.

All this takes place in a soft way without any constraints, since the process is a conjoint discovery, apparently guided by the one asking for help and not by the specialist. This negates resistance to change, since this is not directly requested but indirectly induced.

As will be illustrated with real cases in the next chapter, the reframing paraphrases follow successive groups of strategic questions and gradually shift the attention of the interlocutor from the problem and its persistence to the solution and its necessary manoeuvres.

Such a funnel-like spiral of questions, answers, paraphrases, and confirmations produces a gradual but rapid process of change in the perception of the situation and leads to the modification of the previously used methods of managing it, without directly asking for it or arbitrarily prescribing it.

Evoking sensations

Before convincing the intellect, it is necessary to touch and predispose the heart. "We only consult the ear because the heart is wanting" (1995, *Pensées* I: 30). Once more Pascal, the great persuader, indicates the fundamental importance of evoking sensations to reach the argumentation intended in the persuasive process.

"We can say that you are a sort of broken marionette with its eyes turned towards the inside . . .". This expression evokes an intense sensation in the hypochondriacal person, who is continuously alert for physiological symptoms and thus incapable of relating with the external world. More than any given explanation, this metaphor evokes sensations of how dysfunctional this alertness is and, without impositions, leads the person to want change.

As shown before, conducting dialogue in a strategic way means inducing the interlocutor to change through what he is made to feel; thus, a crucial characteristic is that of making use of evocative language.

All the rhetorical figures of speech and poetic forms may be used with this intent. In fact, there are no linguistic limitations regarding the evoking of sensations within the dialogue. An important factor is that the communicative form should provoke a planned evocative effect in the interlocutor that will be useful in reaching the predetermined aim of the dialogue. In other words, it makes no difference if one makes use of aphorisms or metaphors, anecdotes, or concrete examples, a poetic recitation or a narrative event, an argument or a counter-argument, as long as it evokes a sensation that triggers an emotional effect that leads to the persuasive scope.

For example, one can effectively redefine the situation of desperate solitude by using this image: "You are like an already lit match in the darkness", or by paraphrasing a poetic verse, like Saffo di Leopardi's "even sea water draws back when you get near . . .". Both of these communicative formulations are able to evoke great sensations, which, if used strategically, become corrective.

The art of making use of this technique resides in orientating its effects towards aversive directions about the attitude or behaviour that needs to be interrupted or increased. Thus, evoking sensations should not be a mere literary exercise or an exhibition of an analogical capability in the construction of metaphors, but, rather, a precise rhetorical aspect that hits the interlocutor emotionally to produce the desired reactions.

Thus, with this intent, the formulation should be selected and presented in a way tailored to the communicative style and personal characteristics of the subject. The same formula might be suitable in its presentation on both a verbal and non-verbal level in a way to be felt by the interlocutor as in line with his perception and thus evoke in him an intense sensation. Moreover, one should keep in mind the fact that we should not go against the usual representative system of the subject to be persuaded, otherwise one would produce the very opposite effect. For example, it will not be so effective if we narrate a metaphoric Zen story to rational intellectuals, since these will feel as if we are treating them as banal and ignorant. They would be surely more impressed if we cite a European aphorism. In this regard, in literature one finds various misunderstandings, and usually they make use of metaphors within the therapeutic language without specifying its strategic use. Moreover, they limit the evocative power to the sole narration of stories or use of metaphoric images, while language, with its so varied articulating possibilities, allows the use of many more variants of evocative expression.

In conclusion, the type of communication selected to evoke specific sensations suitable to trigger a therapeutic reaction, besides being tailored to the interlocutor, should be congruent with the personal and relational style of the one who is making deliberate use of it.

If a frail, humble person had to cite an indication taken from the *Art of War*, not only would he not evoke the right sensations but would also appear quite ridiculous and not very credible. The same applies to anyone who cites an aphorism of Oscar Wilde, if cited inadequately. By now it should have become clear to the reader that evoking sensations in a strategic way is a truly difficult technique to follow. It requires prolonged exercise in the use of rhetoric, in recitation, and in the art of stratagem in order to be fully learned and developed as a true personal competence. Otherwise the effect of such a refined and subtle tool of persuasion would be not only inefficient but also counterproductive.

Thus, the persuasive strategist should be able to select the most adequate rhetorical expedient for the specific person and situation to be changed, should introduce it in the most efficient verbal and non-verbal manner, and should use it at the most suitable moments throughout the dialogue. It is clear that all this takes place simultaneously and requires a truly functional communicative ability. After all, the Ancient Greeks already showed great respect for the fact that mastery of art was a technique so refined and practised as to permit the artist to go beyond it.

The strategic dialogue, structured with a sequence of questions, paraphrases, and evocative sentences, is like a musical score that needs to possess its own melody and requires an interpreter able to perform it to its best. Different performers play the same opera differently. Everyone can learn to play the piano and give a good performance of a piece of music, but very few can give shivers to the listeners when touching the keys. Similarly, everyone can learn the technique of the strategic dialogue and use it decently, but very few are those who can turn it into true "art". However, just like those who learn how to play the piano, one can come to delight oneself and others by bettering one's art through years of study and practice. In the same way, if one studies and practises for an adequate span of time, one can learn to put forward strategic questions with the illusion of alternatives, paraphrase the answers while reframing them, and use formulas to evoke sensations. This will allow us to guide our subject towards therapeutic change. Artistic excellence is not a necessary quality of an efficient therapist. In fact, in the majority of the cases, a good technical ability is enough to obtain elevated results. Moreover, there is only one way to become an artist of excellence, by continuously developing one's technical abilities while constantly trying to overcome one's limitations.

Recap in order to redefine

"Ideas transform themselves within us, triumphing over the initial resistance in opposing them and they nourish themselves from already present, rich intellectual reservoirs, which we were unaware that they were destined for this purpose." Marcel Proust (1981), in his celebrated work *Remembrance of Things Past*, indicates how things continuously evolve within us towards new discoveries, which we often realize to be old, forgotten aspects, and reveal unhoped for resources. Such a process, due to its natural inclination, might be used to predispose already present ideas in order to reorganize them. Proust seems to have held the idea that a great talent, rather than originating from intellectual elements and refined social superiority to others, comes from the ability to transform and transpose it.

Once the investigative–discovery phase is completed and new perspectives are induced, one should proceed to recap to give it a *frame* in order to catalyse and consolidate the persuasive process and the acquired change. This summary is proposed as a sort of articulated sequence of the subject's answers. While it clarifies the agreements reached from one phase of the dialogue to another, it is meant to conclusively redefine the joint discovery made about the presenting problem, its persistence, and solutions. However, the latter are not declared directly, but proposed as a logical consequence of the acquired knowledge about how the problem is maintained by what the patient is doing or not doing in their attempt to overcome it. In this way, the patient is led into inescapable change, since this is the inevitable effect of what has been discovered and agreed upon about his discomfort. In fact, this manoeuvre is a sort of super-paraphrase to redefine the entire process of the completed strategic dialogue by constructing a fitting frame. And, just like a perfectly-fitting frame increases the value of a picture, "recap to redefine" frames, consolidates, and catalyses all the previously induced effects, making them come together to produce the changes necessary for the solution of the problem.

The structure of this technique is based on what has already taken place during the session, and, once it is presented in the form of a conclusive paraphrase, it ferments the outcomes by adding a further push towards change, given by this redefinition, which is not only necessary but inevitable. Framing the previous dialogic process with its crucial points within a logical sequence agreed upon by both interlocutors produces a formidable persuasive effect. The psychosocial studies conducted on interpersonal influences (Cialdini, 1984) clearly show that a series of minimal agreements in the sequence can lead to a final important agreement, "getting a foot in the door", i.e., to persuade the person to do something which they probably would not want to do.

"Every little thing leads to another, which then leads to another . . . if you concentrate yourself in doing the smallest thing, then the following and so forth . . . you'll find yourself doing big things by having done only small things . . .". With these words, John Weakland (1993), one of the great masters of brief strategic therapy, guided his pupils (including one of the authors of this book) to focus their efforts on the smallest possible changes during therapy rather than on huge ones, so that through a progressive chain of small but inexorable steps, they will rapidly reach the objective of a big change.

All this brings to mind a maxim of Napoleon Bonaparte: "Since I'm in a rush, I'm going to go slow".

Going back to our premise "recapping in order to redefine", we consider it very important to propose to the patient a conclusive frame of the previous dialogue so that it soundly anchors him and becomes a mnemonic representation of something already fulfilled and not as something that still needs to be acquired. This leads to an operative consequence that will follow, which will be perceived as an effect of known fact and not of a threatening unknown reality.

We are all inclined to *recognize* rather than *to get to know*, because "framing" the unknown with the known reassures us. In the same way, through this manoeuvre, we create a consolidated sensation of reassuring knowledge in respect of the problem and our perception of it, as well as for what is necessary to arrive at its solution. This precious self-deception renders the necessary changes decisively more feasible, increases positive expectations, and boosts the subject's internal locus of control. She will not feel as if she is navigating in the unknown, rather, she feels as if she is partaking in an adventure with precise and reassuring coordinates which will lead her to the desired destination. Although it seems redundant to repeat what has been said so far, at the end of the therapeutic dialogue this ostensible waste of time is in fact decidedly economical and extremely efficient in reaching maximum efficacy through minimum effort. Finally, in summarizing what has been put forward so far in a rhetorical manner also produces strong suggestive effects that further enhance the effect of this manoeuvre because of its hypnotic quality (Servillat, 2004).

Once more it becomes clear how, through this advanced form of the dialogue, one can work contemporaneously on four fundamental psychological levels of the individual: perception, emotion, behaviour, and cognition; all this through a subtle yet elaborated form of *non-directive directivity*.

In fact,

> . . . We must put ourselves in the place of those who are to hear us, and make trial on our own heart of the turn which we give to our discourse in order to see whether one is made for the other, and whether we can assure ourselves that the hearer will be, as it were, forced to surrender [Pascal, 1995: 16]

Prescription as a joint discovery

In *The Waste Land*, T. S. Eliot (1922) writes that at the end of a journey one would find oneself at the starting line. With this poetic image, the author leads us to think that the end of something opens up another thing. This applies also to the strategic dialogue.

Once we arrive at the end of the session, having completed all the phases of the strategic dialogue, we now must weave together all those things done during the interview that produced a change in perspective, so as to turn them into operative actions in the subject's real life. For this purpose, the prescriptive–indicative phase comes to embody a fundamental point, since this is the moment where there is a transformation and a handover of what has been discovered, agreed upon, and redefined during the dialogue. This is the phase of the strategic dialogue that is essentially the same therapeutic style as the brief strategic therapy we were conducting ten years ago. In fact, closing the session by prescribing what the patient should do from one session to the next has remained unchanged, as described in our well-known protocols found in earlier texts. The specific prescriptive injunctions to be put into practice by the patient remain the same, just like those that have been devised and differentiated for each diverse pathology and its variants. One should not forget that without the prior research on the specific forms of therapeutic manoeuvres and tactics for the different forms of pathological disorders, it would not have been possible to study the technical evolution of the dialogue during the first session. It would not have been possible to select the corresponding strategic questions without the previous research that focused on the attempted solutions of each of the different pathologies we studied. Similarly, it would not have been possible to put together the reframing paraphrases or to select the type of language suitable to evoke sensations in a strategic manner, without having identified the specific therapeutic stratagems to unblock patients from the different forms of problem persistence. Thus, the only thing that makes the current prescriptive phase different from that of the past is the dialogue, because it predisposes the interlocutor to more willingly accept the handover of what has been said and put it into practice. In fact, in this way, we see that there lies a clear distinction between the investigative phase (regarding the persistency of the problem) and the injunctive–prescriptive phase (prescriptions that bring about change) in the first session. The entire sequence of the dialogue flows smoothly and naturally to come to the prescriptions that need to be followed. The prescription thus becomes something that is met as a direct effect of what has been previously achieved and agreed upon by both parties. This harmonious evolution of the strategic dialogue makes the prescription not only more acceptable but also inevitable.

CHAPTER THREE

The strategic dialogue in action: examples of technological magic[1]

"The most incomprehensible thing about the world is that it is comprehensible"

(Einstein, 1996, p. 69)

"Advanced technology is in its effects, not so dissimilar to magic." With these words one of the great scholars of the Massachusetts Institute for Technology (MIT), Clarke (in Owen, 2001) shows us that when a technique becomes very refined, its concrete effects might lead us to think that it is magic.

We believe that this applies also in the case of the *strategic dialogue*, when employed against important and resistant forms of psychological pathologies. In order to make it easier for the reader to better understand this rigorous technique, we present in this chapter a number of examples of its application to real cases. A variety of cases were chosen, from the most advanced types of phobic disorders to the most recent specializations of the eating disorders, and to more ordinary problems, drawn from a heterogeneous population (different genders, ages, and of diverse cultural and social backgrounds), which we came across in clinical and public contexts.

The brief comments in italics will help to clarify the advanced strategy of change used, by shedding light on every specific manoeuvre and on the sequence of the problem–solution process. In this way, the reader will immerse himself in the rigorous yet creative art of the strategic dialogue.

Case 1: Dysmorphophobia

Fascinated by the methods of brief psychotherapy, the makers of a well-known Italian television programme about medicine and health proposed an experiment to us to be aired at prime time: a documentary of a psychotherapy session to show the programme's vast audience how complicated human problems can be solved with brief interventions.

The chosen patient was a twenty-three-year-old woman, suffering from a particular problem that is very common in show-business: body dysmorphia. In practice, after having undergone plastic surgery to have silicone implants to increase her breast size, the young woman had once more contacted her surgeon to have her upper lip reshaped. The specialist, highly professional, refused the request, and referred her to another specialist, more suited to the new problem.

Dysmorphophobia is a post-modern phenomenon (Nardone, 2003a), since it is linked to the ever-growing evolution of plastic surgery and the increased social interest in aesthetics. It is based on the actual possibility of undergoing change in certain aspects that so far might have seemed unchangeable, such as physical appearance.

We will proceed to report the actual dialogue between the patient and Professor Nardone.

Therapist: Good morning, Cinzia.

Patient: Good morning

Therapist: May I call you just Cinzia?

To establish a therapeutic relationship

Patient: Why not?

Therapist: Good . . . tell me, what brought you here?

Definition of the problem

Patient: My surgeon referred me here, because I asked him to perform a surgical intervention on my lips. I want fuller lips, but he does not agree that it is necessary.

Therapist: Mm . . . So he told you to come and talk to me!

Patient: Yes.

Therapist: OK. Have you undergone other corrective surgeries or is it your first time?

Questions focused on the attempted solutions

Patient: No, I've already undergone another plastic surgery: I had breast enlargement.

Therapist: OK. Did the intervention go well or have you had any problems?

Patient: No, everything went smoothly. I'm happy with the result.

Therapist: OK, so if I understood well, otherwise please do correct me, you underwent a surgical intervention to correct something physical that you didn't like. It was successful and now you wish to correct another thing, which you feel is not really adequate; it is not the way you want to be.

Reframing paraphrasing: recap to redefine

Patient: Yes, right!

Therapist: The lips.

Patient: Yes, lips.

Therapist: But your surgeon told you, "You don't really need it, so talk to . . ."

Patient: Yes.

Therapist: Mm. OK, and that disturbed you? The fact that he said it is not necessary disturbed you, or it reassured you?

Investigation of the redundant model of the attempted solutions

Patient: No, let's say that I liked it, because . . . from a male point of view . . . he told me I was pretty and that it wasn't necessary. But then . . . I know what I really like or dislike about myself.

Therapist: OK, but, in your opinion it is necessary or unnecessary?

Filtering questions to focus on "the function of the problem"

Patient: In my opinion it is necessary.

Therapist: Before the breast enlargement, were you convinced you had to intervene also on the lips or did this idea come after the breast enlargement?

Patient: Mmm . . . well, it was soon after the breast enlargement.

Therapist: So you discovered a flaw in your lips only after having corrected your other defect?

Recap to redefine

Patient: Yes, that's right.

Therapist: OK . . . what does this make you think? What does this tell you?

Strategic questioning to shift attention on to the dysfunctional perceptive model

Patient: Nothing! [She smiles and eventually starts laughing.]

Therapist: So you found a defect only after you corrected a previous one. Does this tell you anything?

Patient: Well, to tell the truth . . . is this . . . [She smiles once more.]

Therapist: How come you didn't see the defect before, and now you can see it?

Lead the patient to self-discovery

Patient: Well, this is a good question.

Therapist: . . .

Patient: It means that I don't see it any more, because I corrected it and now I look for something else.

Therapist: OK. And do you think that after your lip surgery you would find something new to correct, or it would be enough, you will feel satisfied?

To evoke fear

Patient: I don't know! This is a one-million-dollar question . . . I don't really know.

Therapist: OK, imagine: you correct your upper lip, you become even more beautiful. It works ... Do you think you could see another defect to correct?

Scenario beyond the problem

Patient: No.

Therapist: Why not?

Patient: Because no.

Therapist: OK, in your opinion would a progressive chain of plastic surgeries make you better or worse?

Patient: Psychologically, they make me feel better, because I'm at peace with myself. And for me this is the most important thing, right? Feeling better about myself. I don't really mind about anything else ...

Therapist: OK, so the most important thing to you is correcting defects. Then you feel better about yourself?

Redefine to provoke that which seems unacceptable

Patient: Mind you! No, no.

Therapist: Ah ...

Patient: An entire list of things are important to me, one of which is feeling better about myself, looking at myself in the mirror and feeling happy with how I look.

Therapist: OK, but when you surgically correct a defect, you end up noticing another defect and so you proceed to surgically correct it ... and then you correct another, then you notice another, and so after another ...

Strategic questions based on attempted solutions that feed the problem

Patient: This is not necessarily so. Maybe I can stop here, or go on ... can't really tell.

Therapist: So it is possible, you can stop here, or you can continue? What can make you stop here?

Patient: To stop discovering other defects. [She smiles.]

Therapist: But at present you see the defect in your lips, don't you?

Patient: Well, yes that's right ...!

Therapist: OK, do you know the game of the Chinese boxes? You open a big box and you find a smaller one. Then you open the small one and you find an even smaller one, and a then another one even smaller ... And so on ... I would like you to keep in mind that after every successful corrective surgical intervention, you'll be overwhelmed by the desire to undergo another one ... and then another one ... and so on ... Simply because the surgical correction truly works, this will make you find a new defect to be corrected and a new one ... and so on ... In other words, what I mean, is the corrective intervention that which is making you create new things to be corrected? Do you know Michael Jackson?

Evoke fear: reframing through the use of metaphoric image

Patient: Yes.

Therapist: How many times did he undergo plastic surgery?

Patient: So many times! [She smiles.]

Evoke sensations: associate an unpleasant feeling to what was perceived as pleasant

Therapist: Do you remember? He started with the skin, then the nose, then the entire face ...

Patient: Let's not exaggerate! That's such an extreme case ...!

Therapist: To what extremes he has gone, no? I mentioned this case simply to show you how a good solution sometimes can become a problem, if repeated ...

Redefine to change: to move from the evoked sensation to a new proposed vision

Patient: Hmm ...!

Therapist: Hmm! My advice is start to thinking that correcting your presumed defects can be helpful to you, for sure, but it can become a problem that creates a new problem that will create a new one ... just as in the Chinese boxes game! I used the Michael Jackson image just because it's so strong!

Redefining becomes a jointly agreed upon indication

Patient: Yes! That's true!

Therapist: Please allow me to give you some advice, if I may . . .

Patient: Of course.

Therapist: During the next weeks enjoy looking at yourself in the mirror, five times a day, every three hours for five minutes. Take a pen and paper and note down all the aesthetic defects. Write them down and think how you could correct them. This is a perfect way to avoid the Chinese boxes game, OK?

Direct prescription: a ritual that will bring to saturation and subsequently to a halt the dysfunctional perceptive–reactive model

Patient: OK.

Second encounter

After the session, Professor Nardone and Cinzia meet again for the second time in the television studios. The meeting between therapist and patient during the programme was not in any way preset, thus all that took place was aired without any alteration of the setting.

After a short introduction to summarize the experiment carried out, the programme presenter proceeded to interview the protagonists.

The introduction read:

Prolonging youth is a legitimate aspiration of every one of us. Even if it is only in the way we look, why not . . . but this can become a true obsession. This is the story of Cinzia.

Cinzia is twenty-three and has already had plastic surgery, breast enlargement. However, after this intervention she discovered that she has some other thing that she does not like . . . that is, her upper lip. So she went to the same plastic surgeon, Dr Siniscalco, who told her to wait. In fact, he declared that it would be better to go to another specialist, a psychotherapist, to understand whether this is just a legitimate aspiration to better oneself or whether there is something else. Cinzia then went to Professor Nardone.

We have seen the documentation of the first session of this brief psychotherapy, during which Professor Nardone tries to gather whether there is something else beyond Cinzia's wish to reshape her upper lip. He also gave her a small task, i.e., during the following days to stand in front of the mirror and write down all the things she does not like about herself.

Presenter: [to Cinzia] What did you feel on watching the interview you had with Professor Nardone?

Patient: Well, it impressed me . . . it reminded me of a treasured good moment, because this interview was very important for me.

Presenter: A "good moment"?

Patient: Yes, because it blocked me, blocked the things I thought . . .

Presenter: Excuse me, but it blocked or unblocked the things you thought?

Patient: No, it blocked the things I thought.

Presenter: You mean your decision?

Patient: Yes, my decision. Yes, the decision to undergo plastic surgery to have fuller lips.

Presenter: Ah . . . And why?

Patient: It freed me, unblocked my thoughts. In ten minutes Professor Nardone made me, for the first time, go beyond aesthetic appearance . . . what I could wish or not wish. So, for the moment, everything is suspended, because I'm seriously thinking about it. It impressed me.

Presenter: Listen . . . So what exactly undermined your previous beliefs?

Patient: The fact that I truly didn't see the problem of my lips before the breast enlargement. For me this wasn't a problem and only after the operation this defect came out.

Presenter: Well, I am curious . . . did you carry out the prescriptions?

Patient: No, I didn't, because there was not the need. There wasn't the need at all.

Presenter: Did you take this decision soon after the first session of brief therapy?

Patient: Yes, it impressed me very much . . .!

Presenter: Professor Nardone . . . can you explain better?

Therapist: Well, to carry out a strategic dialogue such as the one you observed is not meant to try to understand but to try to make the person, who has come to us with a problem, perceive it from a different perspective. To create a diverse perception of the same phenomenon will completely change the reaction to, and the respective cognition of, the phenomenon.

Presenter: Change the point of view?

Therapist: Yes, change the point of view. And this through a series of questions that, as you have seen and heard, are particular questions that guide the person through his own answers to change his point of view. Then, through the use of paraphrases that I introduced to confirm this, the new sensations of the person are reinforced.

Presenter: All this in just one session of brief psychotherapy? After this there weren't others?

Therapist: No other.

Presenter: Therefore, let's say that surely Cinzia has reacted in the best way. She was sensible, collaborative, and thus guiding her to feel things in a different way has immediately triggered off what has to be elicited; so well that she did not feel the need to carry out the tasks, the prescriptions given, which were only a reinforcing factor of what had taken place during the session. Generally, after such a session, the majority of patients do not follow the prescription because there is no need, because change has already taken place during the session. If the impact of the session is not so strong, then the prescription is followed.

Now, it is very important to keep in mind the fact that Cinzia came to me when she was still doubting whether intervention was necessary or not, and thus we captured the opportunity which made it easier to find the lever of change. When we have people coming to us after a series of plastic surgical interventions, who continue to be obsessed by undergoing others, or, more accurately, their obsessions are created by the same successive surgical interventions, a single session is certainly not enough. But it is true that the therapeutic intervention can be carried out in a limited number of sessions if one manages to guide the person through a series of questions and answers, together with a paraphrase of his answers, which does not lead to better understanding but to *feeling* differently about something.

In order to schematically summarize the technique of the strategic dialogue as applied to body dysmorphia, it seems useful to put forward a sequential scheme of the used manoeuvres (Figure 1).

Case 2: Managerial depression

While winding up a workshop on communication and strategic problem-solving for managers, and moving on to the application of the technique and of the logic, we asked whether anyone from the public wanted to volunteer and put forward a personal problem.

A brave woman in her forties volunteered, who presented a personal difficulty that influenced both her personal and her professional life. The dialogue took up a research–intervention aspect, and, through the use of strategic questioning, the woman was guided to better clarify the concrete aspects of her problem, especially to herself, and to come to a conclusion or a solution, something which she previously could not see since she was trapped in her rigid perception about the problem.

> Therapist: What is the objective you would like to reach thanks to this possibility?

Definition of the problem

> Patient: Mmm . . . be more decisive . . . in changing work.

> Therapist: Well, what is the difficulty that stops you from doing so, your personal weakness or a situational condition?

> Patient: A personal weakness.

> Therapist: OK. And your personal weakness lies in taking decisions or in fearing the effects of your decision?

> Patient: In fearing the effects of my decision.

> Therapist: Therefore . . . correct me if I'm wrong, in this moment you feel as if you are at a crossroads . . . you should take a decision in changing work but due to your personal weakness

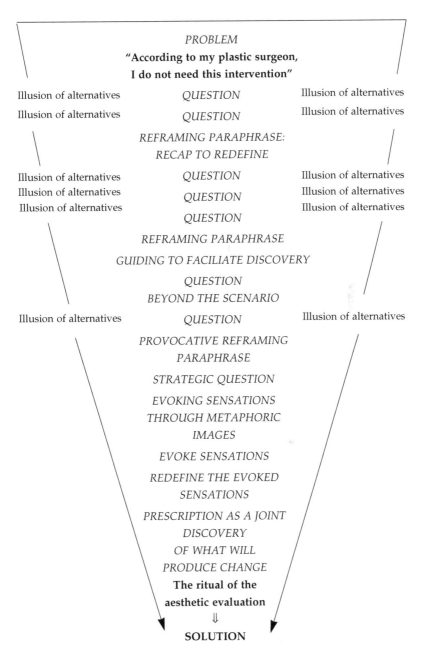

Figure 1. Summarized sequence of the strategic dialogue as applied to body dysmorphia.

you can not manage to do so because you fear the effects of this decision.

Three general questions followed by a summing paraphrase

Patient: Yes.

Therapist: OK. This decision could have bad effects on you only, or also on others?

Investigation of how the problem functions

Patient: Even on others.

Therapist: OK. The effects of this decision would take place in the short-term, immediately, or in the long-term?

Patient: I do not know . . . maybe immediately.

Therapist: Mmm . . . OK.

Patient: But . . . I do not know whether these effects could be called positive or negative.

Therapist: Oh! OK. Very interesting.

Patient: I can foresee which could be the immediate negative effects, maybe in the long term they could be positive.

Therapist: OK . . . Therefore, if I understood clearly, otherwise please do correct me . . . you are there ready to act . . . you need to take a decision but this decision might lead to important effects that in the short term might be negative but in the long term might even be positive . . . However, these negative effects in the short term might affect not only you, but also other persons.

Redefine the problem through paraphrasing

Patient: Yes.

Therapist: And due to these effects you are hesitant.

Patient: Yes, let's say I'm paralysed.

Therapist: OK, OK. And if we had to evaluate the effects of your decisions, mmm . . .? At the moment are you giving more importance to the negative short-term effects or the possible positive long-term effects?

Investigate the perceptive–reactive model

Patient: The negative short-term effects.

Therapist: The negative short-term effects are irreparable, or might they be overcome in a relatively short time?

To create out of nothing

Patient: I do not know! If overcome, that may be not in a relatively short time!

Therapist: Mmm, Therefore, if I'm not wrong . . . otherwise please do correct me . . . at the moment you fear taking a decision that might expose yourself and your loved ones to effects that are rather tough to handle . . . and you are not sure whether you can then remedy these effects in the immediate future or in the long term.

Recap to redefine

Patient: Yes, I hold no certainty that I can remedy the situation in the short term, but maybe in the long term.

Therapist: OK. Therefore, if I'm not wrong, you're sure that you can remedy the effects of your decision, but the immediate situation is that it will bring along negative.

Patient: I'm not sure, but I hold a lot of trust in this, a lot . . .

Therapist: You are not sure, but you hold a lot of trust in this. Your trust in the positive long-term effects is based on the fact that you have real projects, or on your expectation?

Filtering question

Patient: Based on the fact that I have real projects and since I feel there is a lot of unexpressed potential.

Therapist: OK, and this felt potential . . . is unexpressed because your present role at work prevents it, or because you do not manage to express it in your present job?

Patient: Rather the second . . .

Therapist: That is?

Patient: Because I cannot express it.

Therapist: OK . . . Therefore—please correct me if I'm wrong—you are a person who has a problem deciding whether to leave this work or not. You are very worried because there are some negative short-term effects that might influence your life and the life of your loved ones ... these negative effects might persist only in the short term because in the long term you might have other opportunities. And you know this even though you do not hold any certainty, but at the same time you feel that you are jammed from expressing your potential and that this log jam is not due to the situation you are in, but to your incapability to express it.

Redefine through the use of paraphrasing

Patient: Mmm (nods).

Therapist: OK, Please correct me if I'm wrong ... can we thus come to think that if you could manage to overcome this personal blockage, you would be able to change the situation at work without the need of leaving it?

Orientating by making use of the scenario beyond the problem

Patient: I have tried sometimes, and I also had satisfying results. However, this did not last long.

Therapist: OK ... when you tried ... did anything change in you or in others?

Developing premises that will be strengthened in the conclusion: to make the enemy go up the attic and then remove the ladder

Patient: In all spheres, both in me and in others.

Therapist: But where did it start first?

Patient: From me.

Therapist: And you produced effects in others, if I'm not wrong.

Patient: Mmm, mmm (nods).

Therapist: OK, but you said this lasted only a short time! But did you persist in what turned out to be functional, or did you let go because it was tough to keep up?

Patient: I let go.

Therapist: Oh ... please allow me to understand better ... but if I'm not wrong ... if I did not understand wrongly, you have

put into practice certain strategies which proved successful at work ... which might have allowed you to express
your potential. They worked, but after a while you gave
them up and thus the prior situation returned.

Circular reframing of the failed model of the attempted solutions

Patient: Yes (nodding).

Therapist: OK. Please allow me to use quite a strange image ... therefore you are a person who has a problem at work, and is
frustrated because you cannot express your own potential
... in fact you thought, "I need to leave this job, but if I
leave the job, I'll run quite a big risk for myself and my
loved ones." Furthermore, you said that when you underwent certain changes you managed to change the situation
around you ... however, you were not able to maintain
this change in you.

Adding in order to change

Patient: (nods) Yes.

Therapist: OK. Thus, now, do we need to change the organization or
your strategies?

Show the junction that points at a sole direction

Patient: My strategies ... surely!

Therapist: In this moment it is more essential to leave or to change your
ways to keep the job?

Patient: (Pause) In this moment, I feel that it is essential for me to
go.

Therapist: OK, and ...

Patient: Because if this thing had to repeat itself, that is try to
change within that context, if I give up ... there are some
resistances that are not worth ...

Therapist: Resistances from your side or from others?

Patient: From my side, I probably believe it is not worth it ... to
invest so much in this type of context.

Therapist: Oh, OK ... I would like to remind you ...

Patient: So I get tired and that is why I give up.

Therapist: Therefore, if I'm not mistaken, you can change the situation, you have also managed to do so at a certain point, but the fact that you cannot keep up the successful strategy, this causes you to think that it is not worth it.

A redefining paraphrase

Patient: Mmm (nods).

Therapist: OK, did you study Latin at school?

Patient: (nods).

Therapist: Did they ever make you translate the fables of Phaedrus?

Patient: Something, yes . . . (nods).

Therapist: Do you remember the fox and the sour grapes?

Evokes a sensation: reframing her "is it worth it!" attitude using Classics

Patient: (nods).

Therapist: Oh . . . Does it have anything to do with your situation or not?

Patient: (pause). But, no . . . I do not see it in that way.

Therapist: OK, and have you ever thought that . . . that there is a particular rule in life? One can abandon the battlefield only when one is able to stay, to abandon it because one cannot stay, that is called running away, or escaping a situation.

To evoke fear

Patient: (nods). Mmm!

Therapist: Every escape leaves a wound that never heals.

Patient: (pause, then nods). Therefore is it worth insisting and find once more that charge . . .

Therapist: "Is it worth" becoming able to stay so that one can decide whether to leave or to stay? When someone leaves because she is incapable of staying, that's running away, an escape.

Patient: In fact that is why I did not leave, because I understood that I was escaping, running away.

A joint discovery

Therapist: OK . . . and this is an important resource that needs to be exploited . . . and which should be joined to the idea

"I need to change in order to change others" ... You remember what we said before about Gandhi ... "be the change you wish to see in the world". If I want to change others, I need to start to change myself, but I need to keep this up.

Use of aphorisms

Patient:	It's just too tough, I mean ...
Therapist:	Most often life is tough, but ... is it tougher to stay and try to be what you wish others should be or else run away and suffer the effects of your escape?

Illusion of alternatives

Patient:	No, in fact if one had to say ... I think that to run away in certain situations is a courageous act because ...
Therapist:	Hmm, this, please allow me, is usually ...
Patient.	No, but it is true!
Therapist:	And please correct me if I'm mistaken ... OK, you have already said this to yourself? This is the justification or excuse given by those who are not worthy either of a heroic life or of a heroic death ... Do I need to say more or have you already seen the road to follow?
Patient:	Well, yes!
Therapist:	Well, yes! OK. (See Figure 2.)

Case 3: Vomiting

A specialized intervention with an eating disorder specialist.

More often than not, the people who reach the Centre of Strategic Therapy at Arezzo come here as a last resort, when their problem has got worse and more complicated, sometimes also as a result of inadequate therapeutic interventions.

There are numerous and various traps related to the difficult relationship with food and our patient has managed to fall into quite a few of them; her latest was falling for the demonic trap of vomiting, the syndrome where a person eats in order to be able to purge.

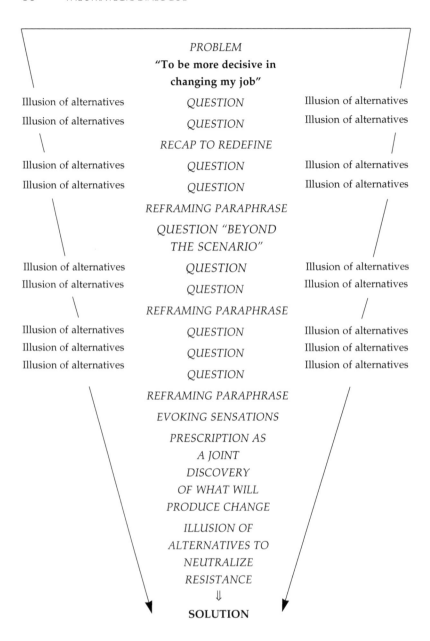

Figure 2. Summarized sequence of the strategic dialogue in dealing with managerial depression..

In this specific case, the therapy was conducted conjointly by Giorgio Nardone and Simona De Antoniis. The dialogue that follows is an excellent example to illustrate how the strategic dialogue can involve not only a single individual but also a whole family.

Co-therapist: What is the problem that brings you here today?

Patient: I read the book, which impressed me . . .

Co-therapist: Yes?

Patient: *Beyond.*

Co-therapist: *Beyond Hate and Love of Food.*

Definition of the problem

Patient: Because I've been suffering from anorexia for many years. I mean . . . before I was much thinner, I was eleven kilos lighter than today. . .

Therapist: Hmm

Patient: Then . . . I underwent psychotherapy. A psychologist that, I must say, has helped me quite a lot but on a psychological level. Everything that related to . . . practical stuff, I mean on my *doubts* about food . . . everything remained unchanged.

Co-therapist: OK, Therefore . . . you have spoken about it?

Patient: Yes.

Co-therapist: The work carried out with the psychologist consisted of speaking, disclosing . . . or did she give you precise tasks to do?

Investigation regarding previous therapies

Patient: No, we spoke, I disclosed.

Co-therapist: OK.

Mother: At the beginning there were tasks for us. Well. to weigh her every three days, but just this!

Father: She gave homework to us.

Therapist: And what homework did she give you?

Mother: Not to be so pressing regarding food. To set her free, as they say . . . in a sense . . .

Patient: I started off by over-controlling my nutrition, sticking to a rigid diet . . .

Therapist: Nearly every one of you [referring to other patients suffering from the same disorder] start off that way, you are not original! (Pause.) Then, how has it evolved over time, I mean you started to lessen your diet or you ate and vomited?

To set out after arriving

Patient: Hmm . . . yes!

Therapist: Well yes! Listen, Roberta, no?

Patient: Yes.

Therapist: Do you eat and vomit usually every day or . . . not always?

A sequence of funnel-like questions to focus the dysfunctional perceptive–reactive model

Patient: No, no. Before it was worse, it used to happen much more often, now it is much less. The problem is that if I'm busy, but I need to occupy every five minutes of my life, so I do not think about it and thus I'm fine. But if I have five minutes where I'm sitting down staring . . .

Therapist: As soon as you relax . . . you are overwhelmed by the urge?

Patient: Yes.

Therapist: And then you will be overwhelmed by the first phase . . . fantasy . . .

Patient: Yes.

Redefine to reframe

Therapist: Then you feel a sort of charge, a drive which leads you to food, to eat, and eat, and eat . . . and then you vomit.

Anticipating technique

Patient: Yes.

Therapist: OK, do you follow this process only once, or at various times?

Focused investigation on how the problem functions: the temporal sequence

Patient: In a day?

Therapist: Yes.

Patient: Various times a day.

Therapist: Various times a day, OK. Therefore you have various episodes of bingeing and vomiting.

Patient: Yes.

Therapist: Are they successive or at intervals?

Redefining the new guided discoveries, step by step

Patient: Successively, and even . . . depends.

Therapist: Your encounters with this "dimension" take place between meals with rituals you have come to construct, or during meals?

Focused investigation of how the problem works: the modality

Patient: Between meals.

Therapist: Therefore you have regular meals . . .

Recapping in order to redefine

Patient: Yes.

Therapist: Highly controlled . . .

Patient: Highly controlled . . .

Therapist: But between meals . . .

Patient: It's a mess!

Therapist: It's a mess! Do you get hold of the food to eat and regurgitate on your own, or do others get it for you?

Patient: No, they do not get it for me . . . I mean, what I find, whatever I find . . . I do not have any . . . I do not go out to buy stuff . . . no!

Mother: I no longer make cakes . . . no more!

Patient: Yes, but it is the same!

Therapist: . . . "it is the same" . . . what do you eat usually?

Focused investigation on how the problem works: the quality of the food

Patient: Anything! I mean, I do not . . .

Therapist: Whatever comes along?

Patient: Whatever comes along, I do not have any preferences. Before it was sweets, now, no . . .

Therapist: OK, Roberta, do you prepare and cook food for yourself or do you eat whatever you find ready?

Patient: Sometimes, yes, depends . . .! Yes, sometimes.

Therapist: It depends how you feel?

Patient: Yes.

Therapist: Do you cook pasta, prepare it . . .?

Patient: Not very elaborate stuff!

Therapist: You just need to stuff yourself. After all, what you like best is to stuff yourself and then empty yourself.

Evoke sensations

Patient: (nods).

Therapist: OK? Fine. [Addressing the parents.] And you, at the moment are you letting things be or you do you, in certain ways, try to intervene?

Investigate the attempted solution of the family

Mother: No, lately she started working at a call centre and is away from home most of the time. Thus . . . I believe that now she does it more often away from home.

Patient: No, I never do so if I'm not at home.

Father: Let's say that now we let her be because it is not so frequent; before it was much more . . . now maybe she listens more . . .

Patient: But it is not that . . . No, besides this, it doesn't matter . . . It is rather that it does not feel comfortable . . . if I want to eat something I do so, but it's just that I do not feel comfortable with food at all! I mean, since I started my controlled diet it seems that all I have to eat is what is allowed, and not more and nothing different from that.

Therapist: And if you go beyond that, you need to eat more and vomit.

Patient: Yes.

Therapist: After all, at that point you know that you have lost control!!

Adding in order to change

Patient: And I do not do so at all . . .

Therapist: But if you lose control, then you vomit?

Patient: If I lose control, yes. I do it very rarely now, I manage to control it just a little better . . .

Therapist: OK Roberta, but as you said before, you usually create your own moments, therefore they are not truly a loss of control but they are looked-for! Correct me if I'm wrong.

Go back to the points mentioned earlier: linear vs. circular

Patient: Yes, well, I do not know! Well, I cannot tell whether they are so. I do not even know myself why . . .

Therapist: OK. What was there in the book that made you decide to come here?

Patient: It is the type of therapy . . . what it does! Especially because in order to solve a problem an individual does not need to look for the causes but rather to look for what he needs to do now in order to solve . . .

Therapist: Did you see yourself in one of the described images?

Patient: Yes, there was a girl . . .

Therapist: OK.

Patient: Yes, not precisely similar . . . a bit of one case and a bit of another. I did not focus on just one person, I just gathered cues from here and there.

Therapist: OK, good. If we had to measure, on a scale from one to ten, how motivated you are to come out of this situation, where do you place yourself?

Patient: At ten.

Therapist: Sure?

Showing disbelief to mobilize and motivate

Patient: Yes.

Therapist: Be careful, I'll test you!

Patient: So many years have gone by! I mean, I have a strong desire to change but I must confess that often I get frightened; however, I do not know, it is as if, oh!, it is as if a part of me is at a halt even though I have a strong desire to come out of this situation. However, there is always something that . . . I call it the tempting devil.

Therapist: Oh, oh. It is a demon that overwhelms you!

To induce fear and to evoke sensation through a metaphoric figure

Patient: Hmm!

Therapist: The temptation . . .

Patient: Yes.

Therapist: Hmm. Well. And that is why I tell you that I do not trust your evaluation score of ten . . .

Patient: In fact, no, I meant ten as a measure of the strong desire . . . that is. Because I believe that there is a double personality in me, when I manage to see things through, I manage to speak about my problems and to disclose how things are.

Therapist: You give yourself the possibility of only two personalities?

Muddying the waters to bring the fish to the surface

Patient: No!

Therapist: You limit yourself so much? Only two?!

Patient: No. I mean that there is a part of me that manages to be focused, then . . . after, however . . .

Therapist: It takes over!

Patient: Yes.

Therapist: When this dimension takes over, the other dimension is suspended, just like Doctor Jekyll and Mr Hyde, and then there is more?

Patient: Then I think . . . for example, especially lately since it's been a while since I last vomited. I mean, I vomit very rarely now, just because I'm filling in every minute of the day. Then, they [her parents] know this: on Saturdays and Sundays I go to the beach, from Monday to Friday I work in Rome, I live on the outskirts so . . .

Therapist: But they are suspicious! They said, "Maybe she does it away from home".

Muddying the waters to make the fish come to the surface

Patient: No. Instead I do not do it if I'm not at home.

Mother: Or maybe when we are away . . .

Father: When we leave her alone at home . . .

Patient: I never do it when away from home . . . never!

Mother: Maybe when we are away . . . because I no longer see her do it. Before, I used to understand when . . . maybe she has become more cunning!

Therapist: Well, to do it better one has to do it in secret. It is much "nicer" . . . am I right?

Evoke sensations

Patient: Even the other psychotherapist told me that if I had to do it I have to do it in secret, that they should not see me.

Therapist: Oh! Well, it is the best way to "perfect" yourself! OK, is this the whole family or do we have other members?

Patient: My brother.

Therapist: Younger or older than you?

Patient: Younger. He is twenty and I'm twenty-six . . .

Therapist: OK. Does he intervene in any way, or does he avoid the subject? (Pause.)

Mother and daughter exchange questioning looks.

Mother: What do you think?

Patient: Well! He is weird, even my brother is weird.

Mother: Now he is in the army . . . he is rarely at home.

Therapist: Well.

Mother: But before, he kept away from this problem. He never pitied her . . . he always kept his distance from this situation.

Patient: He is quite an introvert . . . my brother. So you never know what he might be thinking, you will never know. Maybe he suffers more than others do but he always tries to look . . . dutiful.

Father: However . . . he does suffer. Her situation made him suffer!

Therapist: You said that you are motivated to come out of this situation, true?

Patient: Yes.

Therapeutic double-bind

Therapist: Thus, we want to measure how much you are and we are going to do so in our own style, by giving you precise indications that will allow us to see whether you are a repentant–transgressive or whether you are a gratified–transgressive. We need to understand this, OK?

The stratagem of the revealed stratagem

Therapist: (addressing the parents). But in order to give her these indications, we need to remain alone with her. However, we have an important indication for you: from now until the next time we meet, whatever she does or does not do you need to observe without intervening . . .

Father: That is what we are doing now.

Therapist: What you are already doing? *Observing without intervening?*

Mother: Without revealing sad expressions . . . or happy ones . . .

Therapist: And you should also avoid speaking about the problem. It is all hers.

Mother: Never, we would never speak about it. It is she who often brings it up . . .

Patient: At first it became the centre of our . . . but now . . .

Father: Because the problem was also because she had lost so much weight that she reached a dangerous point, and at that moment . . .

Therapist: True, true. [Addressing the patient.] But that was the other phase, right? That was the abstinent phase; now, at this new phase, these kinds of risks are absent.

Father: The big problem was when she was in that dangerous phase, we were at rock bottom . . .

Patient: But does it happen like that, that you pass from one, from abstinence to, or from . . .?

Therapist: Listen! Saint Augustine—have you read this?—wrote "Abstinence is much easier than moderation" Is it either abstinence or loss of control?

Citing the "great"

Patient: It is true.

Mother: A middle way . . .

Patient: There is no middle way.

Therapist: (addressing the parents). Well, if you will kindly leave the room, I'll come to say goodbye to you later.

Mother: Fine!

Father: Thank you. [Parents leave the room.]

Therapist: But there is something which is not written in the book—OK? The fact that here we do brief focused interventions. Therefore, we will give you ten sessions . . .

Patient: And after that (smiles)?

Therapist: If we do not see any changes, we will dump you. That is, if we do not see changes within the tenth session, that means that our method does not work with you and we do not want to become accomplices of your problem if we cannot help you solve it.

Evoke sensations by arousing fear

Patient: OK , right.

Therapist: You have read that therapy moves along certain given indications or prescriptions. These might seem banal, illogical, grotesque . . .

Patient: I haven't read this!

Therapist: But it should be followed to the letter, OK? Before, I asked you a question, asking you to give a mark from one to ten to show how motivated you are in coming out of this situation. You said ten, now you have to prove this to us!

Patient: OK (nods).

Therapist: But I already told you that I'm rather distrustful about this, because, having met many, many girls like you . . . as you said there is a disparity . . .

Patient: Yes, there is a disparity, that's true!

Therapist: . . . between your will . . .

Patient: . . . and what I can manage to do.

Therapist: It is like a sort of visceral reaction that overwhelms you, hmm?

Patient: Yes, I know.

Therapist: Therefore, allow me to sum up. If we are not mistaken, otherwise please do correct us, you started long time ago with an abstinent anorexic phase, then . . .

Patient: Hmm, I mean . . . now that time has gone by I see things in quite a confusion.

Therapist: Of course!

Patient: That is, I do not have a precise clear vision of what . . .

Therapist: OK, but please do allow me to recap.

Patient: Oh, OK!

Therapist: You started with the controlled diet, then you started to restrict, and then you started to purge. You discovered that you could do something technologically more advanced: eat and vomit. Things got gradually more pleasant, you were caught up in the cycle . . . Recently, it seems that you are putting in great effort towards remaining out of this situation and you have managed to do it less. However, when you had a bit of free time, you ended up doing it again. Am I right?

Recap to redefine

Patient:	Yes.
Therapist:	Therefore, at the moment you can manage not to do it so often simply because you, just like Silvio Pellico, are tied to a chair; since you are doing other things, you cannot do it, but if you had a bit of free time . . . you would do it?

Reframing image
Evoking sensations to transform the perception: from freedom to act to slavery

Patient:	Yes, I would do it!
Therapist:	And you will end up doing it just like before, am I right?
Patient:	I've noticed that recently, unlike before, I have reduced the bingeing. I mean, I eat less stuff, less frequently . . .
Therapist:	Hmm!
Patient:	Then, while before I used to be really "hungry", now I no longer do it because of hunger. I do not know why! Maybe because it became something . . . a habit, I do not know! And only at home!
Therapist:	Of course. There has to be a specific place so as to do it well. OK?

Evoking sensations

Patient:	Yes. I would not do it in any other place.
Therapist:	Therefore, now, in order to see whether you are "repentant" or "gratified", we give you a quite particular task to do, which will be suggested by the co-therapist . . .

The secret is that there is no secret

Co-therapist:	This task is quite particular: we ask you to eat when and how you want, to binge until you feel satisfied. Eat and eat until you feel stuffed. When you feel really good, so good that you cannot take it any longer, in that moment you stop, and, after an hour, you will rush to the toilet and throw up. Therefore, we ask you to continue having your binges as you used to do, when and how it pleases

you, and eat until you feel truly full, stuffed. When you feel that it is the time to go and throw up . . . stop, wait for an hour, then you can vomit . . . OK?

Patient: Do I really need to vomit, at all costs? (Laughs.) Because I'll be sick!

Therapist: We are telling you, but you can choose not to do so . . .

Patient: Of course.

Therapist: However, we know that you do not do it now because you occupy all your time. OK? Just like Ulysses who tied himself to the ship . . . he made others tie him up so as not to fall for the call of the sirens.

Reframing image

Patient: Because, due to my job, I'm away from home most of the day, so I do not think about it!

Therapist: OK, therefore you can choose not to do it if you do not feel like it. But every time you feel like doing it, remember: eat as you please, do not restrain yourself. But when you have eaten and eaten, and eaten, when you feel as if you are about to burst, that you need to rush and vomit . . .

Patient: I need to wait an hour.

Therapist: Look at your watch and wait an hour. Not a minute after or a minute before. When the hour strikes, rush to vomit. Is it clear?

Patient: When I need to vomit, if I do not need to, I do not do it!

Therapist: Of course. It is not an obligation. We leave you free to organize your own life. But every time you eat and vomit, eat as much as you want, OK? But vomit after an hour. Not a minute before or a minute after. And for the entire hour you should avoid eating anything more.

Patient: That is, I have to wait an hour than then vomit.

Therapist: OK.

Patient: If I need to.

Therapist: Without eating or drinking anything further.

Patient: Ah! I should not do anything during the hour.

Therapist: After an hour: exactly. Wait, and after an hour, go and vomit.

Patient: However ... I mean ... one thing. One has to feel the sensation if at home, and that's OK. However, lately, it happened that ... in fact the doctor gave me shots to inject ... I do not know whether it is a consequence, because I cannot seem to vent in "that" way and I need to find other means to do so! I have a sort of panic attack: I feel sick, my blood pressure lowers, I feel breathless and dizzy ...

Therapist: Are they panic attacks or do you believe it is something that has to do with you physically? Or both?

Avoid shifting the focus of the therapy

Patient: That is ... the doctor that visited me, told me that there is something ... fatigue, stress, nervous breakdown ... my nerves ...

Therapist: Oh, OK!! OK, she gave you medication?

Patient: Samir!

Therapist: OK ...

Patient: She gave me Samir. I must confess that it helped.

Therapist: Well ... it is a tonic treatment, therefore it obviously helped! Therefore ... do you remember our prescription?

Patient: Yes. I should eat—perhaps binge one more time—wait an hour, and then purge.

Therapist: Hmm! Then another small thing ... this might be a little bit risky, OK? I would like to insert in your daily diet a very small pleasure, a transgression ...

Patient: (pause). Oh, but transgression for me ... in fact I ... well, let me try to explain: what is that thing I like? What is a transgression for me ... something I could eat ... I have difficulty in choosing, I truly have great difficulties when trying to choose.

Therapist: I believe so, because you have become used to the fact that everything is so controlled. But, you know, we construct our own habits and then our habits construct us. We need to subvert this. To ask you for a small thing, I mean you should choose a small thing that you might like, and then you see whether you like it or not. But every day there should be a small thing . . . OK?

Prescribing as a sort of joint discovery

Patient: OK.

Therapist: Thus, we gave you two tasks, OK? (Figure 3.)

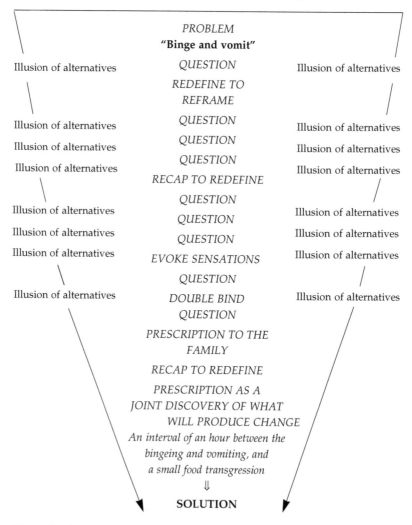

Figure 3. Summarized sequence of the strategic dialogue in dealing with bingeing and vomiting.

The fourth session was carried out after a month at the Centre for Strategic Therapy. During this period of time, the patient was followed-up by the co-therapist. The patient reported that during this month she had been "liberated" from her vomiting, managing to stay at home without being tempted to eat and vomit. This is the full transcription of the fourth session.

Therapist: Please let us know about the situation. Obviously I have been kept informed by her [referring to the co-therapist] but I want to hear it from you.

Patient: Well! I mean . . . I'm fine because I no longer vomit.

Therapist: You never vomited?

Patient: No.

Therapist: Wow!

Patient: I have stayed in . . . at home! Sometimes there were moments . . . but I kept going. At home I was quite agitated but I managed to keep control. I was not over-whelmed by that thing . . . I managed to say "No" and control myself!

Therapist: Wow, how do you explain all this?

Patient: I do not know (laughs). I do not know, but then I noticed that I could eat with more tranquillity!

Therapist: Yes?

Patient: Yes! I have also been to a wedding and I eat—I referred this also to the co-therapist—that is, I do not feel so . . . even when I am looking in the mirror and I feel a bit fatter . . . however, this thought then goes away, I make it go away. It is much easier than before.

Therapist: OK. The people around you, how did they react to such a change? Did they notice this change, after all, or not?

Patient: Yes . . . but they acted as if nothing had happened. I mean, they do not give it such importance. Because even at home I remained quite the same, it isn't that I . . .

Therapist: OK. And this, what has changed in your life?

Patient: I feel more secure. I'm not . . . I gained more confidence in myself.

Therapist:	Hmm. OK. But you never vomited . . . Did you restrict your diet or did you allow yourself the foods as I told you?
Patient:	Yes, I allowed myself . . . especially at breakfast and dinner—I told the co-therapist—a bit less at lunchtime because I did not have so much time for lunch. I do not have so much time to take things easy at lunchtime.
Therapist:	Therefore, you cannot appreciate the taste of good stuff!
Patient:	No, because by two, half past two, I finish at one place and start in another . . .
Therapist:	So you have to rush . . .
Patient:	Yes, I do not have the time, whereas at breakfast and dinner, I'm at home.
Therapist:	. . . so you have started taking care of yourself.
Patient:	Yes. I have a bit more time!
Therapist:	Well. Have you eaten *only and exclusively what you like best*?
Patient:	I eat things I never used to eat: croissants filled with cream, a slice of pizza with ham and mozzarella . . .
Therapist:	Oh! Without being tempted to go and vomit?
Patient:	I went to this wedding. I ate a whole slice and another half-slice of the wedding cake. No! No!
Therapist:	But in this case, did you keep back from . . . or you did not feel like vomiting?
Patient:	No. I mean, I said to myself, now I'm going to the wedding, surely during the meal I would be tormented . . . It was my best friend's wedding! Instead I sat down and I ate . . . did not pay so much attention . . . everything came along so naturally!
Therapist:	Hmm! Well. Hear me out. Therefore, in that moment, the demon, the secret lover . . .
Patient:	Disappeared!
Therapist:	. . . we have locked him in the depths of your castle?
Patient:	Yes. Even though sometimes I still feel it . . . However, I manage to control myself. Where before I failed to control myself, now I have control.

Therapist: Therefore, in this case, if we have to give a mark on the scale from zero to ten, zero standing for when we met—just a month ago—while ten being when you could tell us: "I have solved my problem", what is the mark you would give yourself now?

Patient: I haven't solved my problems hundred per cent; however, for having done so much in just a month, I would give myself seven . . .

Therapist: Seven! Very good. Even I agree with you, I would say.

Patient: This was quite a surprise to me!

Therapist: Really?

Patient: Hmm . . . never thought I would . . . I changed . . . became different.

Therapist: Became different? What do you mean?

Patient: Because you can speak of your suffering only when you no longer live it.

Therapist: Because you feel detached from it?

Patient: Yes.

Therapist: OK.

Patient: Therefore you speak and thus you start to see things differently. You feel more radiant . . .

Therapist: Well . . .

Patient: I like what I'm doing, while before . . . I look in the mirror . . . and I like myself a bit more than before!

Therapist: OK.

Patient: Everything is different!

Therapist: Well, well, Roberta . . . I'm just adding something to what I have said before, then the co-therapist will add other things during your next meetings. The most important thing is that you continue "cultivating" your pleasure in eating by eating only and exclusively the food you like best, in the way you like best. This is the only way to allow yourself pleasure while you can do without the rest. When you did not allow it, the rest became irresistible . . . OK?

Concluding prescription

Patient: (nods).

Therapist: Now we have to pass on from seven to ten. However, we have to go slowly, not rush. The most important thing was to interrupt the vicious circle. Now these three steps from seven to ten, we need to carry them out much slower. OK?

Patient: OK.

Case 4: Panic attacks

The following case is an example of advanced treatment of the panic attack syndrome, carried out at the Centre for Strategic Therapy, conducted by Giorgio Nardone and Simona De Antoniis.

We chose this case among hundreds of resolved cases of panic attack carried out at our institute because it is both an original and an exemplary case. Exemplary because this case clearly reveals the efficacy of the specific protocol designed for the treatment of panic; original because the specific therapeutic process required a particular adaptation, since it involved a couple and not just an individual.

A man in his forties comes to therapy accompanied by his wife. He is the father of two children. For the past thirteen years, he has been suffering from panic attacks and agoraphobia that completely restricted his life. The man was highly engrossed in listening to his physical symptoms with the intent of reducing these threatening sensations, but which resulted in escalating the actual panic. The investigation regarding the "attempted solutions" showed us that, for the past thirteen years, the patient had faced his problem with the help of his wife and organized his entire life in a way to limit exposure, to protect himself. Therefore, in this case, the panic attack persisted due to the attempted solutions—total avoidance and requests for help—that each time confirmed to the man his incapability of overcoming this problem. Once more, the problem complicated itself due to the attempts used to solve it.

Right from the very first session, we worked on making the man break free from this dependency, so as to discover his own resources.

Stopping the attempted solution of the family, together with introducing a new type of interaction between the couple, will gradually help to bring the patient to construct his own personal, social, and professional potential, which so far had been blocked because of the problem. He will be autonomous from the entire family system and, moreover, will fend for himself so as to construct a personal equilibrium and establish self-confidence.

Co-therapist: What is the problem that brings you to us?

Patient: I'm the problem! For the past thirteen years I've been suffering from panic attacks, this is my problem. It has evolved in various ways, in various types of panic attacks ... For a while I was afraid of some things ... another time I was afraid of other things, but the result was always the same: panic attack, and a need to run away from the place I'm in ... the classical type of panic attack.

Therapist: Oh, oh! Well, you can start [referring to the co-thera-pist].

Co-therapist: But precisely what used to take place?

Definition of the problem

Patient: Precisely, I get really agitated.

Therapist: Oh!

Patient: Strongly agitated ...

Co-therapist: Tachycardia, sweating ...?

Anticipation technique

Patient: Yes, in fact lately, for example, my head feels lighter ...

Therapist: What do you mean by "my head feels lighter"?

The wise man fakes being stupid

Patient: What do I mean?

Therapist: As if your head flies away?

Patient: As if ...

Therapist: It breaks away from your body and wanders away?

Patient: No!

Therapist: Oh!

Patient:	However . . . it feels as if it wanders off, as if I'm going through a dizzy spell . . .
Therapist:	Ah, OK.
Patient:	I'm afraid of this dizzy spell and . . .
Wife:	That something more will happen!
Therapist:	OK, OK. But are you afraid that you will die of a sudden death or . . .?

A sequence of funnel-like questions to understand the perceptive–reactive model

Patient:	Yes, that I might die!
Therapist:	. . . or do you fear losing control and losing your sanity? What is your fear, at that very moment, when you are overwhelmed by the panic attack?
Patient:	No, rather than of losing my sanity I fear . . .
Therapist:	. . . dying.
Patient:	Dying!
Therapist:	OK. Well . . . you enter a sort of tunnel . . .
Patient:	Yes.
Therapist:	Before you have your panic attack; OK? Does this usually take place in situations you can predict, or can the attacks take place wherever, in unpredictable situations?
Patient:	Lately, they take place when I have to face something!
Therapist:	Oh! Can you give us an example?
Patient:	Well, an example, an example . . . [looks at his wife]
Wife:	For example, at the office.
Patient:	At the office: we have a motorization company. In the morning we have to go to the licensing office to carry out . . .
Therapist:	Yes.
Patient:	Lately I'm finding it difficult to go to this office, thus, I get strongly agitated.

Therapist: In that case, if I'm not wrong, you fear exposing yourself to this situation?

Patient: Yes.

Therapist: OK! But in that case do you fear having to face people or the fact that you have to wait there for long? Which of the two?

Patient: Maybe both!

Therapist: And, usually, do you tend to avoid or face the situations you fear?

A sequence of funnel-like questions to understand the attempted solutions

Wife: He avoids!

Patient: I've been avoiding, but I must say that the very few times I face the situations I manage to overcome them . . .

Therapist: Uh!

Patient: I feel fantastic. I feel good!

Co-therapist: I believe so! [Everyone laughs.]

Patient: I feel like going back to the place, to face it once more, so as to . . .

Therapist: . . . but at the same time you tend to avoid . . .

Patient: Yes, lately I do: I cannot manage!

Therapist: Therefore, if I'm not mistaken, you are a person who has panic attacks, linked with a great terror of undergoing some sort of electrical shock that can kill you.

Reframing paraphrasing: recap to redefine

Patient: Yes, in fact . . . exactly so!

Therapist: And this takes place in specific situations . . . and now that you've learned which they are, you tend to avoid them . . .

Patient: Yes.

Therapist: Even if you know that if you face it you feel good afterwards . . . you still tend to avoid?

Patient: Yes.

Therapist: Do you tend mostly to avoid, or to ask to be helped, to be accompanied . . . by her?

Patient: Hmm, maybe to be accompanied by her . . .

Focus on the request of help that maintains the problem

Therapist: OK!

Wife: However!

Patient: However, sometimes . . .

Wife: However, since I cannot accompany him all the time, we have two kids . . .

Therapist: Hmm!

Wife: Oh! Let's say we have overcome this, at least at work . . . my brother carries out all the errands at work.

Patient: I have employed her brother to go to these places, while I do other things.

Therapist: Fantastic . . . so you organize yourselves very well, eh?

Being ironic about the attempted solution of the family
[Everybody laughs.]

Patient: A person tends to create . . . his own world . . . even though it is not true, so as to protect himself, even though it is not true . . .

Therapist: Hmm!

Patient: It is even worse! Because now I know, I understand that!

Therapist: OK . . . however, you say to yourself "I'm not able, so what can I do . . . I understand this does not help but I cannot do otherwise and then I feel worse!"

Use the first person to declare the interlocutor's point of view

Patient: In fact there are moments when . . . I'm able to face the situation and I feel good for a whole month, month and a half . . . however, afterwards I relapse, I'm not able to . . .

Therapist: OK!

Patient: I'm not able to always feel good. This is the problem!

Therapist: OK. But before you came here, had you tried out other therapies or not?

Investigate previous therapies

Patient:	In thirteen years, I just had one session.
Wife:	Two!
Patient:	Two sessions! At ... a neurologist? In Salerno ... then I saw you on TV in the Costanzo Show (popular Italian talk-show), I've read your book, and I convinced myself to come to you!
Therapist:	Oh, OK! Therefore, in thirteen years you never underwent therapy.
Patient:	No!
Therapist:	You have just organized yourself.
Patient:	Yes.
Therapist:	Well done!

Being ironic about the failed attempted solution
[Everybody bursts out laughing]

Wife:	So ...
Therapist:	Go ahead!
Wife:	But I have to say ... I do not know ... just to ...
Therapist:	Uh!
Wife:	Everything started, in my opinion when he ... we were still engaged and he went to Milan ...
Patient:	For work!
Wife:	In fact everything started then!
Patient:	Eh! Everything started then!
Wife:	He was recovering from high blood pressure, 200, and the doctor said that such a high blood pressure could lead to a stroke. Everything triggered off from then!
Patient:	"Be careful, you might have a stroke soon!" and that was my end. This is what happened ...
Wife:	Then he came back. He came back and from then the whole thing triggered off, even though I've noticed things have got better. Before, he used to shut down his office and

come home; he is no longer doing this. If he feels bad and he is alone, he manages . . . to continue . . .

Patient: Even though I must confess I do not feel good, by the by!

Therapist: OK, thus, if you are in a secure place, such as the office, even though you are overwhelmed by fear you still manage to control it.

Recap to redefine

Patient: Yes.

Therapist: But if you had to go to those places that frighten you, you would not manage?

Patient: No, I would not manage! Not even to line up in a queue, not even if I had to take a coffee at the bar! I'm not able to!

Wife: Let me give you some examples: before coming here we went to a toy shop to buy toys to . . ..

Therapist: Hmm!

Wife: We did not take time to choose, we bought the first things we saw.

Patient: I told her to hurry up, because I could not take it!! Eh, Eh!

Therapist: OK. At that very moment when you say "I cannot take it", OK, do you tend to listen to your body, your rising symptoms, or do you feel observed by others?

To enter the perception of fear through questions that eliminate ambiguity

Patient: At that very moment I feel heady . . .

Therapist: Your head in the clouds . . . Metaphorically you are just like a sort of broken marionette with its eyes turned inwards; always looking at what is happening on the inside.

Reframing by using a metaphoric image

Patient: Yes.

Therapist: And those who look for something, find something.

Patient: Those who look for something, find something. I invent my own illnesses, high blood pressure, all these . . .

Therapist: Well!

Patient: I create these symptoms that create fear . . .

Therapist: Therefore . . . therefore. I have to say that what you have told us makes us understand that we can help you. Better still, as you have heard and read, this is the type of problem we have treated mostly in recent years; therefore, I believe we have the instruments to help you, and quite rapidly at that, but we do not know whether you would be able to follow us in the treatment. You have read my book and you might have seen that the treatment entails prescriptions to be carried out, prescriptions that might appear banal, or illogical, but which need to be followed to the letter.

Patient: Yes.

Therapist: OK?

Patient: OK.

Therapist: The other rule, which is not clearly stated in the book but which is implicit, is that we give ourselves a limited time; we give ourselves ten sessions, not one more if we do not see results. This means that if, by the tenth session, we do not see any changes, we interrupt therapy. If we cannot help you to solve your problem, we do not want to become accomplices of your problem, but I have to say—as you must have read—with this type of problem, this never takes place.

Patient: Yes!

Therapist: Rather, in the majority of the cases, the problem solves itself well before the end of the ten sessions, but we do not know whether this will be so in your case? Let's see!

Patient: Hope so!

Therapist: Well, well. Let's see whether we can transform the broken marionette into a mended marionette, which looks to the outside and not to the inside, OK? We have two tasks for you, the co-therapist will give you one, I will give you the other.

Agree on the objective by using a metaphoric image

Patient: Yes.

Therapist:	In the meantime, I will give you a table that will help you follow the indications given by the co-therapist.
Patient:	Yes.
Co-therapist:	Well, what we are about to ask from you is to bring to us a sort of photograph of what happens to you in your critical moments. Precisely in that moment when you feel fear arising, that you start to feel sick, you take this paper and write down your sensations . . .
Therapist:	You already have the table! You should transcribe that into a small notepad, OK?
Patient:	Yes. [Reads.] Date, place, and persons, situation and thoughts . . . symptoms and reactions.
Therapist:	Well!
Co-therapist:	Symptoms and reactions. You have to fill in all those things at the very moment you start feeling that you are about to have one of your crises: we need to have a snapshot: we do not need you to write it after it happens, because that would be a reconstruction . . .
Patient:	When I feel that soon I will be having my panic attack, in that very moment . . .
Therapist:	Well . . .
Patient:	I stop and I write!
Therapist:	—and write. Then, in two weeks' time, we have a series of snapshot images of all those moments. This will help us to understand how it works and what we should do to change it. Therefore, the more precise you are, the more you can help us to help you. Please! [Referring to the wife, who wanted to add something.]
Wife:	I'm sorry, in case this happens, for example, in the office, and he is alone with a client . . .
Therapist:	You say "Excuse me but I have to write down something regarding work . . ." Invent something! He has no idea what you are doing . . . does he?
Patient:	Sure!
Therapist:	You get hold of a nice notepad, we call it the "captain's logbook". You carry it with you in your pocket every-

where you go, ready to be used: if there is a client with you, just say, "Excuse me, but I have to jot down something otherwise I will forget . . .!". I do it all the time; I say, "Oh, I have to write something down otherwise I'll forget . . .!"

Patient: And I write it down?

Therapist: Yes, at that very moment, OK?

Patient: Yes.

Therapist: The other important task involves both of you. From now until the next time we meet, you should take up a sort of *conspiracy of silence* regarding this problem, or, better, you should start thinking that the more you speak about it the more you feed it . . . Fear is one of our constructions that, the more we speak about it, not only does it not help but we make it worse. The majority of people think that the more you speak about it the more you feel relieved. But in fact it is as if you pour a special fertilizer on to a plant: it makes it grow excessively, bigger and bigger. Therefore, you should keep a sort of conspiracy of silence, OK?

Prescription to the family: conspiracy of silence and to observe without intervening

Patient: That is avoid speaking?

Therapist: Avoid speaking.

Patient: Avoid speaking.

Wife: So if I understand that . . .

Therapist: You should be afraid to speak about it. If you speak about it, you feed it.

Wife: So, if I understand, he and I have to act as if nothing is happening.

Therapist: Yes, observe without intervening. That's it . . . OK? Moreover, I would like you [referring to the patient] to ask yourself a question every day. The question might seem strange, but it is this: "If I want to voluntarily worsen my disorder, instead of bettering it, what do I need to do or not do, think or not to think, to voluntarily worsen my symptoms?"

"How to worsen" prescription: in order to straighten something first I have to learn how to bend it even more

Patient: That is if I want to feel worse?

Therapist: How can you rationally programme the situation to make it worse? What do you need to do or not do, to think or not think to voluntarily worsen the situation?

Patient: You are asking me this?

Therapist: Yes. It is the question you should ask yourself every day and then bring us the answers. The logic of the question is "If I want to straighten something, first I need to know all the ways I can bend it even more".

Patient: Yes!

Therapist: Obviously the question is theoretical, thus the answers should be theoretical. You have already done well in complicating the situation, ok?

Patient: Yes.

Therapist: Thus, just limit yourself to theoretical answers, OK? Therefore you have the "how to worsen" question, the "conspiracy of silence", and the logbook, OK?

Patient: Yes.

Therapist: See you in two weeks' time. (Figure 4).

Second session

Therapist: So, how are things?

Patient: Things are quite fine.

Therapist: What does this mean?

Patient: It means, hmm ... that by doing these new things, by writing down on the paper as soon as I feel the panic coming ...

Therapist: Hmm!

Patient: ... I never had an actual panic attack.

Therapist: No, you never had a single panic attack?

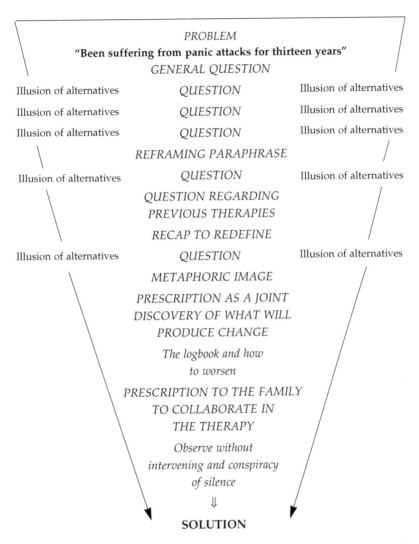

Figure 4. Summarized sequence of the strategic dialogue for dealing with panic attacks.

Patient: Never once did I have a panic attack.

Therapist: Not even once?

Patient: No!

Therapist: Therefore we are happy!

Patient: Good!

Therapist: And what type of life did you lead? Did you continue avoiding certain places?

Patient: Well, yes!

Therapist: Oh, well, nobody told you to do otherwise!

Patient: However, especially during the first days after we came here, I was slightly more serene . . . inside! This is what happened.

Therapist: Uh . . .

Patient: Then, work, stress . . . these increased, so this internal serenity started lessening, but I still managed to find it through writing!

Therapist: Ah. Therefore, there were critical moments but not panic attacks?

Patient: No panic attacks.

Therapist: Oh! Let's see!

Patient: On two or three occasions, I felt really good soon after I wrote!

Therapist: Oh! Well, Well, did you bring your logbook? The things you wrote?

Patient: Yes, yes. I have them.

Therapist: Therefore, when you wrote, even those critical moments seemed to melt away . . .

Patient: Yes. Yet anxiety remains!

Therapist: We should not ask too much from providence . . .

Patient: Yes, however . . . this has never happened before.

Therapist: Ah, OK. Providence helps us, but we cannot ask too much from it, otherwise we would be greedy . . .

Patient: I apologize for my handwriting.

Therapist: It's fine. [Looking through the logbook.] Well, well, well . . . therefore, every time you wrote, it passed.

Patient: Yes.

Therapist: Well, therefore you must have come to notice that this task was not only diagnostic, but it was already therapeutic.

Patient: Sure, sure! Just like a small vent. . .

Therapist: Hmm . . . as if to settle the score!

Patient: What?

Therapist: As if to settle the score with fear.

Patient: Ah, yes, yes, yes!

Therapist: Fear looked in the face . . .

Patient: . . . looked in the face!

Therapist: Well, well. I made you settle the score and look fear in the face and write it down . . .

Patient: Yes.

Therapist: Very good! However, you never had moments of true panic? They never took place . . .

Patient: No, as soon as I started feeling them coming, I practically . . . blocked them.

Therapist: Well, well, anything to add? [Turning to the wife.]

Wife: There were times where I noticed that something was happening; other times I didn't.

Therapist: Is that true, you did not even notice anything?

Wife: Sometimes I didn't.

Therapist: Uh, well! You still kept on being so present, so protective with him . . .

Wife: No, no, I avoided speaking . . . as you told us.

Therapist: Ah, hmm! So you avoided speaking about it?

Patient: Yes, yes, yes! Until now!

Therapist: Was this difficult or easy to do?

Wife: No.

Patient: No, only one . . . but what's wrong in asking . . . "How do you see me?" I mean . . . just to . . .

Wife: To see what I think!

Patient: Just to see whether I have changed . . . I do not know!

Therapist: Ah, and what did she tell you?

Wife: I told him that sometimes I noticed [that he was having a panic], but . . . that he started reacting differently than before.

Therapist: OK. Well, I'm very pleased! Did anything happen to you that would have normally made you go into a panic state, but instead you didn't?

Patient: No, I mean . . .

Wife: However, he has been to the hairdresser.

Patient: Yes, I went to . . . I faced it!

Therapist: OK!

Patient: I faced it and . . .

Therapist: Therefore you avoided certain situations?

Wife: Yes.

Patient: Yes, but not always. Other times I just avoided . . .

Therapist: Of course! However, nobody asked you to test yourself, isn't that so?

Patient: However, I will do this . . .

Therapist: Sure! Very good indeed.

Wife: For example, he never used to go to the barber . . .

Therapist: But?

Wife: No, he was never pleased to go, he tried to avoid that, instead . . .

Therapist: Ah!

Wife: This time he went.

Patient: Well, just a couple of times, however . . .

Wife: Well, yet you did go!

Therapist: And what were the answers to the question we gave you? The second task . . .

Patient: The second task was not to speak and then to think, once a day . . .

Therapist: How to worsen . . .

Patient: That is, what were those things that would have triggered my panic throughout the day. I did not manage to think about it every day, I mean, there were times when I forgot. Oh, hmm . . . logically, I forgot a couple of times . . . but the times I thought about it I faced certain things in a different way . . .

Therapist: Oh, yes? Which were these things that came to your mind, which can voluntarily worsen the situation. What did you have to do to worsen the situation?

Patient: Go to certain places . . .

Therapist: OK, well . . .

Patient: Do certain things at work, or rather go to certain places . . .

Therapist: OK.

Patient: I should be able to go alone . . .

Therapist: Hmm!

Patient: It is then when I feel blocked!

Therapist: Uh!

Patient: And thus . . . let's say in this time I've been to various places, thinking about work, I managed . . .

Therapist: Ah! So you did do certain things you wouldn't have done before?

Patient: Yes, Yes, I did! I was also glad to . . .

Therapist: . . . to do so!

Patient: To do so because they happened, they were not planned, and I was glad that they happened because this gave me the opportunity to face them . . .

Therapist: Well, well, well. Therefore, in reality, not only did you not have panic attacks, not only by writing did you manage to melt away anxiety or fear, but you also did things you would have avoided before . . . certain things!

Patient:	Certain things!
Therapist:	Good. OK?
Patient:	However, this does not mean that all my anxiety is gone, eh?
Therapist:	Slow . . . slow down.
Wife:	In the first days, he felt "charged"!
Therapist:	That would have been too much, this would have meant that he came here for a miracle and I'm not yet so close to our blessed God, OK?
Patient:	Yes.
Therapist:	Well, well. Thus, as I usually say in such cases, it is as if we have unblocked a jammed mechanism, now we have to make it work . . .

Therapy continued for another eight sessions, following to the letter the treatment protocol of panic attacks (Nardone 1993, 2000, 2003), until the presented problem reached complete resolution, i.e., the patient's acquisition of complete personal autonomy.

In this case, as in the majority of the cases, after the strategic dialogue developed in the first session, the specifically-designed therapy for this particular disorder was carried out, which is made up of a sequence of therapeutic techniques and stratagems constructed *ad hoc* to block this type of pathological persistence. It is important to note that, just as in the majority of the cases, thanks to the strategic dialogue, the initial invalidating symptoms disappeared soon after the first encounter. Therefore, the successive phases of therapy take place on the dramatic yet surprising (for the patient) changes achieved during the first session. This shows clearly how such a beginning, which seems quite magical, makes it easier to guide the patient to recover his personal resources.

After this full immersion in *the strategic dialogue in action*, we believe it is useful to shift the attention of our readers on to certain key points.

First, even though the structure of the questions and the paraphrasing can be constructed *ad hoc* for each specific class of problems and its respective most common, redundant dysfunctional attempted solutions, they need to be fitted and adapted to the person and the specific context. Furthermore, within the same pathology, we might find different variants that require different orientation of the dialogue. In this regard, at our Centre, work is in progress to systemize all the different questions, paraphrasing, and evocative manoeuvres that are the most suitable internal differentiations within the already studied pathologies. Parallel to this there is an ongoing empirical observation to formulate structured dialogues for other pathologies (Servillat, 2004).

Second, it is important to demonstrate the non-verbal aspect of the dialogue, which cannot be expressed fully in the transcriptions of the therapeutic dialogues and the comments thereon, but which holds a fundamental role because it amplifies, gives a frame to, and creates ambivalence in relation to verbal communication. It was not by chance that right from the very beginning of our research study on clinical interventions and in our training programmes, we made use of video recording systems, which became the main instrument not only for observation but also for training purposes. In fact, our students, thanks to the videotapes of the sessions in which they progressively participate more actively, are able to watch themselves, evaluate, and compare their therapeutic performance with that of their supervisor, who sits right there next to them throughout the session. In this way, the student who is learning the technique gradually comes to correct his mistakes, both in the strategy and in the communication, at first by imitating the "master" until he finds the master in himself.

Note

1. This chapter was edited by Simona De Antoniis.

CHAPTER FOUR

A dialogue on the dialogue

"It is through the combination of dissonant features that the most beautiful harmonies emerge"

(Epicurus, in Messner Loebs, 2003)

In order to conclude to our exposition we felt it would be useful and, we hope, appreciated by the reader, to put forward a dialogue between the two authors of this book, obviously related to the strategic dialogue.

The difference here is that in this dialogue, the two authors, who are like two expert warriors who exchange roles in attacking and defending in order to train themselves in the best possible way to create a sort of harmonic and scenographic dance, both put forward questions, give answers, and propose paraphrases so as to redefine the content of the dialogue.

Nardone: Dear Alessandro, I believe that you more than anybody else, in virtue of your long experience as an emeritus scholar of psychology and psychotherapy, can guide me to understand whether this technique is truly something innovative or is just a distorted idea of somebody, i.e. me, who is so much involved in it.

Salvini: Surely, it would be too rushed to say that what seems immediately innovative in the method you propose is the fact that it renders, in any case, the interlocutor *active* in respect to what is said and done, because change implies an *active*, not a "passive" or "reactive" individual. In fact, the leap between the old and the new forms of psychotherapy consists of this: the passage from a deterministic scheme—where the other is the product of his genes, his education, his family, his past experiences, his personality traits—to a pragmatic scheme, where the subject is in any case the constructor of his reality through his concrete and symbolic interaction with himself, others, and the world.

As we have stated on previous occasions, "pragmatic" does not mean "practical". According to Dewey (1916) and James (1890), this means a diverse way of looking at psychological problems. What the patient says about himself, feels and perceives, relates and acts, is always the result of an interpretative process of a single mode of manipulating his story. His narrative of the truth exploits and manipulates the historical, distorting it towards a certain direction and meaning. In the case of pathologies, these are the dysfunctional and redundant attempts to control or solve the problem. In this sense, the strategic dialogue, with its focus on getting to know a problem through its solution, represents, undeniably, an epistemological evolution.

Moreover, in line with the pragmatic tradition, this model takes up a position that regards the patient as a person whose ideas and feelings are not limited to mere reflection of his psycho-biographic reality or the actual facts and conditioning he has undergone, but are factors that the person transforms and elaborates to produce an "experience" and a consequent way of perceiving and acting on things. Thus, the strategic therapist is first and foremost a psychologist or psychiatrist who has changed the way of thinking by passing through a positivist empiricist to a pragmatic paradigm, or, rather, to an "interactionism" free from a physicist, aprioristic, factual, deterministic hindrance.

Often, in contrast to what one might think, it is the psychologist and psychiatrist who are resistant to this paradigmatic leap; their cognitive resistances are functional to keep up their identity in line with the social expectancies of the role they hold. One can pour new knowledge into a vase but the new knowledge will not modify the vase, or, more likely, the former will take the shape of the latter.

A further innovative characteristic of this technique is that this type of dialogue differentiates itself from other communicative methods used in psychotherapy, because it is a true and proper strategic intervention, where the subject is led to a take up the point of view suggested by the therapist. For example, he accepts that the attempted solutions have dysfunctional effects, and the natural tendency, without being told so directly, is that of wanting to change this. This dialogue between the therapist and the patient is a very particular form of communication. In syntheses, we can say that it is a co-construction of reality, where the subject is unaware but actively involved. It consists of leading the other to convince himself that he is seeing things through a perspective that in reality is suggested by the therapist through a funnel-like, dualistic stratagem of questions and answers.

These questions have a double task, that of making the patient aware of how he confronts his reality while at the same time leading him to choose from antagonistic options, a diverse mode of "configuring" it. The successive paraphrases will anchor these assumptions as truly lived experiences. All this leads to an effective change in the mode of perceiving things. In other words, if the person is a victim of self-deception, he can be cured through another self-deception. A characteristic of this way of conducting a therapeutic dialogue, which is truly innovative, is that of transforming the patient's pathogenic self-deceptions, of which he is the actual artificer.

Nardone: According to your point of view as a sceptic scholar, is the change acquired in such a rapid way by this type of therapeutic dialogue radical and persistent over time, or is it a superficial change that after a while will be followed by relapses, by a return to the patient's old pathogenic model?

Salvini: Well, dear Giorgio, human psychological problems are particular problems. The way they are generated and might be solved implies a diverse way of thinking from that used to solve physical problems. Individuals are active subjects who construct events which they then have to endure. Their level of reality is inscribed not only in concrete experience, but also in the explicit or inexplicit loquacious propositions that produce real effects, that structure in a dialogical mode the organization of thoughts. These confer to the produced reality a certain tangibility that follows the same direction and meaning given by the subject. The key to change, therefore, is to lead the person to modify his point of view in respect to the problem he is suffering from: perceptions, evaluations, causal attributions, meaning given, loquacious terms . . . Changing perspective triggers off a change on all these levels, which, besides producing rapid and concrete effects, will stabilize itself. If the invented, or, better, the reconstructed, is thus channelled, it becomes credible and thus is felt as true. Without being aware of this, the interlocutor will find a coherence from what has been said, affirmed, and felt, thus reorganizing his perception of reality in a structural manner.

Nardone: Would you define this modality of conducting a dialogue as a manipulative technique, or a strategy to induce therapeutic collaboration?

Salvini: The strategic dialogue seems to be an array of therapeutic stratagems, thus something different from a consultancy, from an exhortative conversation, from descriptive or explicative communication. In this case, as Austin affirms, "to say is therefore to act".

Therefore, the therapist does not explain, but acts by saying, by utilizing the answers of the interlocutor. It is a strategic interaction, therefore a particular way of managing a dialogic rapport, with persuasive and reframing effects. The dialogic scheme constructed in autonomy, or, more accurately, the dialogue that guides the interlocutor along a path of *alternatives* where one excludes the other, uses and follows a logical conception of reality which is divided into opposites; a concept that is fundamental in Western culture. The effect is a soft manipulation, which is simplified but not reductive. This helps to reduce the complexity, to introduce the interlocutor to a path that will help to exploit the persuasive possibility to the maximum based on the principle of coherence, which exploits in a conventional and elementary way the representation of reality through opposites. Nobody can tolerate or violate the principle of non-contradiction, if this is introduced as a rule in an argument. It is not validity, the truth of the scheme, which is of interest, but that of gaining self-persuasive effects; in order to get around and defend an argument, it is necessary to avail oneself of an argumentative scheme, that holds a highly reassuring logic because it already makes part of the thinking mode of the interlocutor. Thanks to all this, we discover something that infringes the previous models of perception of reality, leading them to self-destruction.

Nardone: Well, Alessandro, to paraphrase all your answers . . . please correct me if I'm wrong, but you seem to consider the strategic dialogue an innovative technique that is the natural evolution of the brief strategic psychotherapy model that has been originated and developed by the Centre of Strategic Therapy during the past fifteen years. This is a tradition that has shifted from pragmatism through symbolical interactionalism to the formulation of the School of Palo Alto.

Furthermore, if I'm not mistaken, you believe that the effects of this strategy are therapeutic; they are radical changes and not a sort of therapeutic amalgam of a person's perception, representations, and behaviour. Such therapeutic effects tend to persist over time because they affect the modality through which each one of us constructs what we then have to endure.

Finally, it seems clear to you that this communicative exchange is not a manipulative directive forced upon the patient, but a subtle induction to a therapeutic self-deception that triggers a virtuous spiral of conjoint discoveries between the therapist and the patient.

Salvini: Yes, truly so. I see that you have gathered very well what I think! What does changing one's point of view imply, solely changing the cognition or changing one's actions?

Nardone: From my point of view, changing cognition . . . on the contrary, to what the traditional forms of psychotherapy, orientated towards insight and therefore towards the prevailing work on incrementing the cognitive structure of the patient, might have conveyed . . . cognition represents only the ultimate and not even the most important therapeutic effect. When a person is led to change his point of view in respect to a reality that he cannot manage, the first effect we get is of a perceptive type, or, rather, we change the way he feels about something. The second effect is to

translate the different sensations produced by the diverse perceptions into actions.

Only through carrying out these two phases will the necessary
changes to solve the problem be orientated towards the acquisition
of awareness of all this. Changing point of view presents an illuminating discovery. The discoveries, in the most realistic terms, cannot
be carried out on a cognitive level. Cognition is an effect and not
the cause of a discovery.

Salvini: Is the strategic dialogue a method applicable only to
certain types of disorders, or to all known pathologies?

Nardone: Nothing applies for everything or forever. If it were the
case, it would be an inhuman act. The technique of the strategic
dialogue, like brief strategic psychotherapy, is a problem-solving
model which, by definition, might be applied to all typologies of
problems but which requires a constant form of adaptation to the
specific context, situation, and person. Furthermore, it is revealed to
be, without doubt, most efficacious in certain classes of disorders
where the suffered symptomatology incapacitates the person, such
as in the case of phobic and obsessive compulsive disorders, eating
disorders, presumed psychosis, conflicting relationships, etc. It was
not so significantly efficacious with other forms of therapeutic
dialogue based on explanations rather than injunctions, and with
psychological discomforts with no acute disorders. The emerging
paradox is that the briefest forms of therapy are most suitable for
the highly difficult and resistant pathologies.

Salvini: Are the dysfunctional attempted solutions considered to
be a sort of symptomatological effect of a personality disorder, or as
factors that play or have played an important function for the
person?

Nardone: The concept of the attempted solution, elaborated by the
research group of the Mental Research Institute of Palo Alto, refers
to the redundant modality that might be observed in a person,
given as a response to a specific problematic situation. Thus, these
are forms of interaction between the subject and his reality that over
time turn into a rigid script that the person tends to repeat. In the
empirical research carried out in our centre during these past fifteen
years to formulate specific treatment protocols for specific patholo-

gies, we observed that certain scripts with failed attempted solutions are similar for different individuals suffering from the same pathology. Thus, it is not the personality of the suffering subject that determines the pathogenic attempted solution, but the organization of the problem that structures similar answers even in different persons. This also indicates that certain redundant modalities that aim to manage the problem tend to establish a form of equilibrium that resists change and forms around itself a whole series of other equilibria that are interdependent, which, at some point, will render it functional or, better still, useful. For example, for a person suffering from a phobic disorder who continuously asks for help from his partner or mother in order to be able to confront threatening situations, the persistent use of this script will, over time, structure a morbid relationship between the person and his privileged helper. Thus, having a problem becomes a sort of advantage.

Salvini: Dear Giorgio ... let's paraphrase together your answers. Please correct me if I'm wrong, but from what you said, it seems important to repeat, using Austin's words, "to say is to act"; the thought transferred into the words becomes an action, and thus it constitutes an experience that, if well-focused, becomes self-corrective.

You believe, if I understood clearly, that this form of the strategic dialogue is applicable to all psychological dysfunctions. However, it is up to the therapist's ability to bring to a halt the problem, not only as a symptom but also the representations, the mental organizations, and the behaviours that the person uses in a recurring way to manage his problems.

Finally, if I'm not mistaken, you believe that the secondary advantages that are constructed on the bases of the pathological dynamics become important in the organization of the person, even though they are dysfunctional. For example, certain relationships remain stable thanks to the persistence of a symptom. Research shows that such symptomatic expressions, or, better, the redundant scripts of dysfunctional attempted solutions, are not caused by alterations in the subject's personality, but are the result of the effect of the subject's dysfunctional interactions with situations that activated pathogenic perceptions and reactions, which, over time, became a true and proper pathology.

Nardone: That's right. I'm pleased to hear that you have understood my idea so well!

Salvini: Please allow me, Giorgio, to wrap up with a reflection that I would like to propose to the reader. All that has been described in this text might seem cynical, sophistic, tricky, and so forth, but in this case (in a de-ontological reality which is highly controlled and professionally qualified) the joint aim of the therapist and the patient justifies the means. In surgery this is a recurrent standard procedure to give back the patient his health, which might be described as "manipulative", "devious" (tricky), etc. It is looking at things, assuming an implicit moral judgement on the use of words, to find the metaphysical truth. Even an elementary school teacher manipulates the attention of his students. He manipulates their minds by making them concentrate on certain notions and not on others. In certain cases, it is necessary to take away the words from the moralizing shadow of their recurrent use. Even the word, "cynical": its original lexical meaning is "a way of thinking and of acting in which holds a certain distrust towards rules, habits, and conventions imposed by tradition (*nomos*)". The Cynics were proponents of a sober, anti-conventional mode of thinking, drawn to cultivate the ethic as a personal conquest. This then became a true life style and a way of thinking. Antisthenes, Talete, and Lucian of Samostata, to cite a few, are among those Cynics that have undergone instrumentally moralized judgement on behalf of other schools of philosophy; they were especially forced into confession as demanded by the religious and political authority, i.e., to follow the aprioristic and authoritarian definition of how an individual should perceive and act. The psychological dysfunctions (which we usually call psychopathologies) are the offspring of an authoritarian and dogmatic mode of generating reality which, due to this, the person tends to limit to a single expression its meanings and actions, to render it pervasive, redundant, and a generator of failed attempted solutions. We can, therefore, recognize the value of the strategic dialogue not only in the ancient Sophistic tradition but also in the Cynic school. The negative sense—instrumental and improper—of the terms "sophist" and "cynic" becomes irrelevant. The strategic dialogue that we have described so far, in line with these traditions, not only guides the person to discover how to solve his problems, but also helps him invent his own freedom from the rigid pathogenic and normative traps typical of ideological visions. Among its various powerful exponents, we find the traditional forms of psychiatric-ism. Ancient and modern history teaches us that this is one of the most recurring examples.

Nardone: What you seem to express in such a passionate way, not only does it enthuse me but it brings to my mind the words of three thinkers. This is the best way I can use to associate myself with what you have affirmed.

The first of the three thinkers is Francis Bacon (1690), who regards mental traps as a form of rigid schemes created by humans who need to give to the world more order and regularity than it actually has.

The second thinker is William James (1890), who warns us of the risks of tying ourselves to reassuring descriptive theories. He invites us to use these theories not as point of arrival but as a spring-board, since they are instruments in our research and not the answers to our enigmas.

Finally, the words of the philosopher Epictetus (1955), who invites us to put aside trying to understand the causes and to identify the perpetrator of a situation if we yearn to find the solution to the problem or to change a reality constructively. He stated that to accuse others of their own miseries is a proof of human ignorance; to accuse oneself denotes an initiation of understanding; while to stop accusing others and oneself denotes true wisdom.

Salvini & Nardone: Isn't this the best way to bring to an end our dialogue on the strategic dialogue?

REFERENCES

Abbagnano, N. (1993). *Storia della Filosofia*. Turin: Utet.

Altshuller, G. (2000). *The Innovation Algorithm*. Worcester: Technical Innovation Center.

Alexander, F., & French, T. M. (1946). *Psychoanalytic Therapy*. New York: Ronald Press.

Anonymous (1990). *136 stratagemmi. L'arte cinese di vincere*. Naples: Guida Editore.

Aristotle (1924). Rhetoric. In: W. D. Ross (Ed.), *The Works of Aristotle*, W. R. Roberts (Trans.). Oxford: Clarendon.

Aristotle [(2004). *Sophistic Refutations*. W. A. Pickard (Trans.). Cambridge: Kessinger.

Astin, A. E. (1978). *Cato: The Censor*. Oxford: Clarendon.

Austin, J. L. (1962). *How To Do Things with Words*. Cambridge, MA: Harvard University Press.

Bacon, F. (1690). *Novum organum sive indicia vera de interpretatione naturae. Opere filosofiche*. Bari: Laterza, 1965.

Bateson, G. (1972). *Steps to an Ecology of Mind*. New York: Ballantine.

Bateson, G. (1980). *Mind and Nature*. New York: Bantam.

Berti, E. (1987). *Contraddizione e dialettica negli antichi e nei moderni*. Palermo: L'Epos.

Boorstin, D. J. (1983). *The Discoverers: A History of Man's Search to Know His World and Himself*. New York: Random House.

Cialdini, R. B. (1984). *Influence: How and Why People Agree to Things*. New York: Morrow.

Cioran, E. (1993). *Sillogisme dell'amarezza*. Milan: Adelphi.

Clarke, A. C. (2001). In: N. Owen (Ed.), *The Magic of Metaphor*. Crown.

da Vinci, L. (2004). *Aforismi*. Florence: Giunti.

Dewey, J. (1916). *Democracy and Education*. New York: Free Press.

Descartes, R. (1637). *Discourse on Method*. London: Penguin Classics, 1973.

Diels, H., & Kranz, W. (1934–1937). *Die Fragmente der Vorsokratiker*. Berlin: Griechish und Deutsch Trad. Italian edition: *I presocratici: testimonianze e frammenti*. Bari: Editori Laterza.

Diogene Laerzio IX, 51 (1983). *Vita dei filosofi*, Vol I. Bari: Laterza.

Einstein, A. (1996). *Bite-size Einstein. Quotations on Just About Everything from the Greatest Mind of the Twentieth Century*. J Mayer & J. Holmes (Eds.). New York: St Martin's Press.

Eliot, T. S. (1922). *The Waste Land*. New York: Boni & Liveright.

Elster, J. (1979). *Ulysses and the Sirens*. Cambridge: Cambridge University Press.

Epictetus (1955). *Enchiridion*. G. Long (Trans.). New York: Prometheus.

Erickson, M. H., Rossi, E. L., & Rossi, S. I. (1979). *Hypnotic Realities: The Induction of Clinical Hypnosis and Forms of Indirect Suggestion*. New York: Irvington.

Freud, S. (1933a) *New Introductory Lectures on Psycho-Analysis*. S.E., 22: 3–182. London: Hogarth.

Galilei, G. (1999). *Dialogo sopra i due massimi sistemi, Tolemaico e Copernicano*. Florence: Casa Editrice Leo S. Olschk.

Goffman, E. (1969). *Strategic Interaction*. Philadelphia, PA: University of Pennsylvania Press.

Helman, H. (2001). *Great Feuds in Medicine: Ten of the Liveliest Disputes Ever*. New York: Wiley.

Hendricks, R. (1989). *Lao-Tzu: Te-Tao Ching*. New York: Ballantine.

Hubble, M., Miller, B., & Duncan, S. (1999). *The Heart and Soul of Change: What Works in Therapy*. Washington, DC: American Psychological Association.

James, W. (1890). *The Principles of Psychology*. New York: Henry Holt [reprinted: Harvard University Press, 1983].

Jullien, F. (1998). *Traité de l'efficacité*. Paris: Grasset & Fasquelle.

Kant, I. (1996). *Critique of Practical Reason*. M. Gregor (Ed.). Cambridge: Cambridge University Press.

Locke, J. (1849). *An Essay Concerning Human Understanding*. Oxford: Oxford University Press.

Loriedo, C. (2001). Personal communication.

Loriedo, C., Nardone, G., Watzlawick, P., & Zeig, J. K. (2002). *Strategie e stratagemmi nella psicoterapia. Tecniche ipnotiche e non ipnotiche per la soluzione, in tempi brevi, di problemi complessi*. Milan: Franco Angeli.

Mead, G. H. (1966). *Mind, Self and Society*. Chicago, IL: University of Chicago Press.

Messner Loebs, W. F. (2003). *Epicurus: The Sage*. Harvard University Press.

Nardone, G. (1991). *Suggestione Ristrutturazione = Cambiamento l'approccio strategico e costruttivista alla psicoterapia breve*. Milan: Giuffrè.

Nardone, G. (1993). *Paura Panico, Fobie*. Florence: Ponte alle Grazie.

Nardone, G. (1994). *Manuale di sopravvivenza per psicopazienti, ovvero come evitare le trappole della psichiatria e della psicoterapia*. Florence: Ponte alle Grazie.

Nardone, G. (2000). *Oltre i limiti della Paura*. Milan: Rizzoli.

Nardone, G. (2003a). *Non c'è notte che non veda giorno*. Milan: Ponte alle Grazie.

Nardone, G. (2003b). *Cavalcare la propria tigre*. Milan: Ponte alle Grazie.

Nardone, G. (2004). Constructivist theory and therapy. In: J. Sommers-Flanagan & R. Sommers-Flanagan (Eds.), *Counseling and Psychotherapy Theories in Context and Practice* (pp. 376–392). Hoboken, NJ: Wiley.

Nardone, G., & Cagnoni, F. (2002). *Perversioni in rete. Le psicopatologie da internet e il loro trattamento*. Milan: Ponte alle Grazie.

Nardone, G., & Domenella, R. G. (1994). Processi di persuasione e psicoterapia. In: *Scienze dell'interazione* (pp. 67–79). Florence: Angelo Pontecorboli Editore.

Nardone, G., & Fiorenza, A. (1995). *L'intervento strategico nei contesti educativi. Comunicazione e problem-solving per i problemi scolastici*. Milan: Giuffrè Editore.

Nardone, G., & Portelli, C. (2005). *Knowing Through Changing: The Evolution of Brief Strategic Therapy*. Carmarthen: Crown.

Nardone, G., & Watzlawick, P. (1993). *The Art of Change*. San Franciso, CA: Jossey-Bass.

Nardone, G., & Watzlawick, P. (2005). *Brief Strategic Therapy*. New York: Rowman & Littlefield.

Nardone, G., Giannotti, E., & Rocchi, R. (2001). *Modelli di famiglia. Conoscere e risolvere i problemi tra genitori e figli*. Milan: Ponte alle Grazie (English edition in press).

Nardone, G., Milanese, R., Mariotti, E., & Fiorenza, A. (2000). *La terapia dell'azienda malata. Problem solving strategico per organizzazioni*. Milan: Ponte alle Grazie.

Nardone, G., Verbitz, T., & Milanese, R. (2005). *Prison of Food: Research and Treatment of Eating Disorders*. London: Karnac.

Nietzsche, F. (1974). *The Gay Science*. W. Kaufman (Trans.) New York: Random House.

Pascal, B. (1995). *Pensées*. A. J. Krailsheimer (Trans.). London: Penguin Classics.

Pessoa, F. (1993). *Maschere e paradossi*. Milan: Feltrinelli.

Plato (1955). *The Republic*. D. Lee (Trans.). London: Penguin Classics.

Plato (1989). *Symposium*. A. Nehamas & P. Woodruff (Trans.). Indianapolis: IN: Hackett.

Plutarch (1916). *Parallel Lives*. B. Perrin (Trans.). Cambridge, MA: Harvard University Press, Loeb Classical Library.

Plutarch (2002–2003). *Delphic Dialogue*. R. Lamberton (Ed.). New Haven, CT: Yale University Press.

Proust, M. (1981). *Remembrance of Things Past*. S. Moncrieff (Trans.). New York: Random House.

Reale, G. (2000). Platone, tutti gli scritti. Milan: Bompiani.

Rogers, C. (1951). *Client-centered Therapy*. Boston, MA: Houghton Mifflin.

Roncoroni, F. (Ed.) (2003). *La saggezza degli antichi*. Milan: Mondatori.

Russell, B. (1940). *The Philosophy of Santayana*. Evanston, IL: Northwestern University Press, The Library of Living Philosophers.

Russell, B. (1950). *Unpopular Essays*. London: George Allen & Unwin [revised edition London: Routledge, 1995, reprinted 2002].

Salvini, A. (2004). *Psicologia Clinica*. Padua: Upsel.

Santayana, G. (1905–1906). *The Life of Reason*. D. M. Cory (Ed.). New York: C. Scribner's Sons.

Servillat, T. (2004). First session hypnotic questioning. *Brief Strategic and Systemic Therapy European Review*, 1: 165.

Severino, E. (1984). *La filosofia antica*. Milan: BUR.

Scruton, R. (1997). *Guida filosofica per tipi intelligenti*. Milan: Raffaello Cortina Editore.

Sirigatti, S. (1999). Personal communication.

Skorjanec, B. (2000). *Il linguaggio della terapia breve*. Milan: Ponte alla Grazia.

Smiley, T. (Ed.) (1995). *Philosophical Dialogues: Plato, Hume, Wittgenstein: Dawes Hicks Lectures on Philosophy*. Oxford: Oxford University Press for the British Academy.

St Thomas Aquinas (1920). *The Summa Theologica of St Thomas Aquinas.* Fathers of the English Dominican Province (Trans.). London: Benziger Brothers.

Sun Tzu (1995). In: Sun Pin, *Military Methods.* Boulder, CO: Westview Press.

Thom, R. (1989). *Structural Stability and Morphogenesis: An Outline of a General Theory of Models.* Boston, MA: Addison-Wesley.

Volpi, F. (Ed.) (1991). *L'arte di ottenere ragione.* Milan: Adelphi.

Von Foerster, H. (1993). On constructing a reality. In: W. F. E. Preiser (Ed.), *Environmental Design Research,* Vol. 2 (pp. 35–46). Stroudsburg: Dowden, Hutchinson & Ross.

Watzlawick, P. (1977). *Die Möglichkeit des Andersseins: zur Technick der therapeutischen Kommunikation.* Bern: Hans Huber.

Watzlawick, P. (1984). *The Invented Reality.* New York: W. W. Norton.

Watzlawick, P., & Nardone, G. (Eds.) (1997). *Terapia Breve Strategica.* Milan: Cortina.

Watzlawick, P., & Weakland, J. (1977). *The Interactional View.* New York: W. W. Norton.

Watzlawick, P., Beavin, J. H., & Jackson, D. D. (1967). *Pragmatics of Human Communication: A Study of Interactional Patterns, Pathologies and Paradoxes.* New York: W. W. Norton.

Watzlawick, P., Weakland, J., & Fisch, R. (1974). *Change: Principles of Problem Formation and Problem Solution.* New York: W. W. Norton.

Weakland, J. (1993). Conversation—but what kind? In: S. Gilligan & R. Price (Eds.), *Therapeutic Conversation.* New York: W. W. Norton.

Weakland, J. H., Fisch, R., Watzlawick, P., & Bordin, A. M. (1974). Brief therapy: focused problem resolution. *Family Process,* 13(2): 141–168.

Whitehead, A. N. (1947). *The Wit and Wisdom of Alfred North Whitehead.* Introductory Essay by A. H. Johnson (Ed.). Boston, MA: Beacon Press.

Whitehead, A. N., & Russell, B. (1910–1913). *Principia Mathematica.* Cambridge: Cambridge University Press.

Wilde, O. (1997). *Sayings of Oscar Wilde.* London: Gerald Duckworth.

Wittgenstein, L. (1980). *Remarks on the Philosophy of Psychology.* Oxford: Basil Blackwell.

Xenophon (1923). *Memorabilia: Oeconomicus Symposium apology.* E. C. Marchant & O. J. Todd (Trans.). Cambridge, MA: Harvard University Press, Loeb Classical Library.

INDEX

Abbagnano, N., 2
absolutist ideology, 6
Alexander, F., 113
Altshuller, G., 35, 113
Anonymous, 113
aphorism(s), 3, 24, 42–43, 65
Aristotle, 7–8, 113
art of argumentation, stratagems,
    xi, 2, 5, 9, 27, 30, 34, 42–43, 50
    see also: communication,
    rhetoric, therapeutic
    techniques
  Eristic, 2
  Maieutic, 5–6
assessment questions, xiv
Astin, A. E., 13, 113
attempted solution, 14, 21–22, 25,
    30, 38, 40–41, 48, 51, 53, 63, 70,
    84, 87–89, 100, 105, 108–110
Austin, J. L., 13, 106, 109, 113

Bacon, F., 11, 111, 113
Bateson, G., 12–13, 113

Beavin, J. H., 117
Berti, E., 113
Bonaparte, N., 46
Boorstin, D. J., 5, 7, 10, 114
Bordin, A. M., 14, 117

Cagnoni, F., 14, 115
case studies
  Cinzia (dysmorphophobia),
    50–59
  eating disorder patient
    (vomiting), 65, 67–84
  female manager (managerial
    depression), 58–66
  patient suffering panic attacks,
    84–100
Catholic
  church, 8–9
  hereafter, 10
Centre of Strategic Therapy,
    Arezzo, xi, xiii, 65, 107
chessboard example, 28–29
Christian, 2, 8, 35

Cialdini, R. B., 45, 114
Cioran, E., 4, 114
Clarke A. C., 49, 114
communication, xi–xii, 1–2, 12–13,
    24, 26, 34, 36, 43, 58, 101,
    105–106 *see also*: art of
    argumentation, rhetoric,
    therapeutic techniques
    persuasive, 1
    sophistry/Sophistic, 2–4, 8, 12,
    110
Copernican theory, 9–10

da Vinci, L., 114
Democritus, 3
Descartes, R., 35, 114
Dewey, J., 104, 114
Diels, H., 3, 114
Diogene Laerzio, 3, 114
Domenella, R. G., 34, 115
Duncan, S., 21, 114
dysfunctional script(s), 38, 40,
    108–109

eating disorder(s), 14, 49, 65, 67–84,
    108 *see also*: case studies
    strategic dialogue on, 67–84
Einstein, A., 11, 33, 49, 114
Eliot, T. S., 47, 114
Elster, J., 10, 114
emotionally corrective experience,
    38
Epictetus, 111, 114
Epicurus, 1, 103
Erickson, M. H., 12, 36, 114
Eriksonian hypotheses, ix
evoking sensations, 22, 24, 26,
    42–44, 48, 52, 54, 59, 64, 66, 70,
    72–73, 75, 77, 80

feeling and understanding, 23
Fiorenza, A., 14, 34, 115–116
first session, xii, xiv, 16, 24, 27,
    47–48, 55–56, 84, 100
Fisch, R., 14, 117
free association(s), 11

French, T. M., 113
Freud, S., 11, 114

Galilei, G., 9–10, 114
Giannotti, E., 14, 115
God, 7, 10, 35
    and the devil (dialogues
    between), 2, 8
Goffman, E., 12, 114
Gorge, 4–5

Helman, H., 11, 114
Hendricks, R., 30, 114
Herodotus, 7
homework, *see*: therapeutic
    prescriptions
Hubble, M., 21, 114
hypnosis/hypnotic language, 12,
    46

illusion of alternatives, 8–10, 16, 26,
    33, 36–39, 41, 44, 59, 66, 80, 95
interactional–stragic therapy/thera-
    pists, 13

Jackson, D. D., 117
James, W., 11–12, 35, 104, 111, 115
Jullien, F., 37, 115

Kant, I., 33, 114
Kranz, W., 3, 114

Locke, J., 11, 115
Loriedo, C., 14, 35–36, 115
Lucian, 7, 110

magic/magical, xii, xiv, 49, 100
    power of words, 11
managerial consulting, xiii–xiv, 14,
    34, 58–64, 66
managerial depression, *see*: case
    studies
Mariotti, E., 34, 116
Mead, G. H., 12, 115
mental trap, 36, 111
Messner Loebs, W. F., 1, 103, 115

metaphor/metaphoric, 3, 42–43, 54, 59, 72, 90–91, 95
Milanese, R., 14, 34, 116
Miller, B., 21, 114
mirroring technique, 12

Nardone, G., 10, 13–15, 30, 34, 36, 50, 55–57, 67, 84, 100, 103, 105–108, 110–111, 115
Nietzsche, F., 4, 116

obsessive disorder(s), 14, 108

panic attacks, 16–17, 24, 27, 79, 84–100 *see also*: case studies
    strategic dialogue on, 85–100
Pascal, B., 10, 25, 34, 39–40, 42, 47, 116
Pessoa, F., 24, 26, 116
phobic disorder(s), 14, 49, 108–109
    see also: case studies
    strategic dialogue on, 50–55,
Plato, 5–7, 116
platonic
    dialogues, 7
    love, 6–7
    tyranny, 11
Plutarch, 7, 116
Portelli, C., 15, 115
pragmatism, 12
process of discovery, 23, 25
Protagoras, 2–4, 34
Proust, M., 39, 44–45, 116
psychoanalytic dialogue, 11
psychotherapy/psychotherapies, 11–12, 15, 23, 30, 67, 103–105
    brief strategic, xi, 50, 55–57, 107–108
psychotic disorders, 13, 108
Ptolemaic theory, 9
Pythagoras, 37
Pythagorean Theorem, 6

questions/questioning, 2, 4, 6, 9, 13, 16–24, 27, 28–29, 33–41, 44, 47,

51–53, 57–61, 66, 80, 86–87, 90, 93–95, 98, 100–101, 103, 105

Rationalism, 4
Reale, G., 116
reality/realities, xii, 5, 12–14, 25, 27, 35–36, 39, 46, 104–111
recapping (in order to redefine), 24, 44–46, 51–52, 59, 61, 66, 69, 76–77, 80, 87, 90, 95
reframing paraphrases, 18, 20–24, 27, 39–42, 44–45, 48, 51, 58–60, 62, 64, 66, 87, 95, 101, 103, 105, 107, 109
religious dialogue, 9
rhetoric/rhetorical device, stratagem, xi, 1–2, 4–9, 11, 15, 34, 42–43, 46 *see also*: art of argumentation
Rocchi, R., 14, 115
Rogers, C., 12, 116
Roncoroni, F., 6, 37, 116
Rossi, E. L., 12, 36, 114
Rossi, S. I., 12, 36, 114
Russell, B., 1, 7, 116

Salvini, A., 104–111, 116
Santayana, G., 1, 116
scientific dialogue, 9
Scruton, R., 116
Servillat, T., 46, 101, 116
Severino, E., 116
Sirigatti, S., 30, 116
Skorjanec, B., 116
Smiley, T., 116
Socrates/Socratic, 4–6
St Thomas Aquinas, 9, 35, 117
Sun Tzu, 117

Talete, 33, 110
the "egg of Columbus", 29–30
Theory of Relativity, 11
theory of reminiscence, 6
therapeutic change, xii–xiii, 15, 44

therapeutic prescriptions, xiv,
    25–26, 36, 47–48, 55–57, 59, 66,
    75, 79, 80, 84, 91, 93–95
therapeutic
    techniques/stratagems/
    communication, xi–xiii, 12–16,
    20, 25–26, 34, 36–37, 43, 46–48,
    100–101, 105, 107
Thom, R., 38, 117
true–false, 7
truth, 6–8, 10, 40, 104, 106
    absolute, 7–8, 11
    metaphysical, 6, 110
    of the "Scholastic Philosophy", 8
    scientific, 9

Verbitz, T., 14, 116
Volpi, F., 2, 117
Von Foerster, H., 1, 14,
    117

Watzlawick, P., 13–15, 25, 34,
    36, 115–117
Weakland, J., 13–14, 117
Whitehead, A. N., 5, 117
Wilde, O., 43, 117
Wittgenstein, L., 30, 117

Xenophon, 117

Zeig, J. K., 14, 115